Is Ritalin the Answer?

D0478156

If your automobile

- won't start
- gets only 6 miles to the gallon
- sputters, shakes and knocks
- puts out blue smoke

wouldn't you check on the type and quality of fuel you are putting in your car's gas tank?

Shouldn't we also look at the "fuel" being put in children's "gas tanks?"

It is easy to see why the harassed teacher of a disruptive, inattentive child would call the parents and say, "Something has got to be done about Johnny."

It's easy to understand how a stressed mother and father who've been trying to cope with an ADHD child at home would call the physician and say, "Please help us."

It's also easy to see why the physician who prescribes Ritalin does so because it helps many children with ADHD settle down and pay attention.

Ritalin does provide temporary relief for the symptoms of 65-70% of the children with ADHD just as aspirin helps many people with headaches.

Yet, medication for each of these common problems should not be continued indefinitely without searching for the causes.

Your Child with ADHD
Resembles A Jigsaw Puzzle

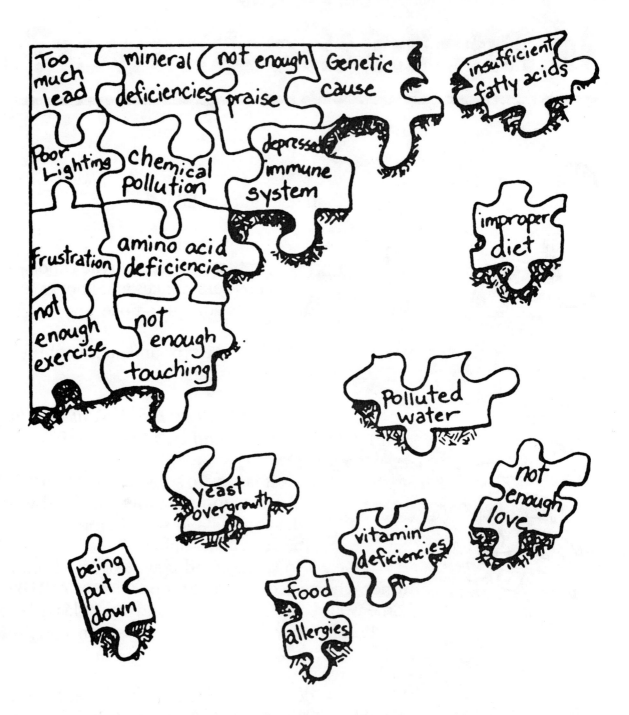

This book will help you put the pieces of the puzzle in place. And when you do, chance are good that your child will not require Ritalin.

Ritalin helps many children settle down and pay attention. No doubt about it!

THE COMMERCIAL APPEAL
MEMPHIS, THURSDAY, FEBRUARY 29, 1996

Ritalin given to 10% of U.S. boys, ages 6-14

The New York Times News Service

UNITED NATIONS — In a report released Wednesday, an international narcotics agency documents a dramatic increase in the use of a stimulant drug to temper children's behavior, and says the drug could pose dangers to their well-being and lead to addiction when improperly used.

The wide-ranging survey of general drug use worldwide by the Vienna-based International Narcotics Control Board said that methylphenidate is be prescribed for 3 percent percent of all American s children to control vaguely defined attention cit disorders.

Because most of th dren are male, this r 10 percent to 12 pe U.S. boys between 14 are on the dru cials believe.

"According t ADD may be

Copyright (c) 1996 by The New York Times Company. Reprinted by permission.

production and trafficking worldwide, including:
■ The use of synthetic drugs known as amphetamines — among claim... manuf... "ice stasy Brit Phi il'

The Virginian-Pilot
WEDNESDAY NOVEMBER 20, 1996

Doctor tracks heavy Ritalin use at schools

Attention-deficit prescriptions are nearly twice the national average in 2 area systems.

BY DEBRA GORDON
STAFF WRITER

Ph... tim...

Th... in e... Ports... dren... low the...

For y... of medic... ...ervices for Portsmouth public schools, has seen a steady increase in the number of children who take the medications for attention deficit hyperactivity disorders. Now she has statistics.

Used with permission.

rades 2 through 5 — 17 percent takes medication for ADHD h day, according to recently ased data.

e analysis, conducted by psy-gist Gretchen LeFever of Nor-Center for Pediatric Research, d identical numbers for the Virginia Beach school system.

Overall, 10 percent of Virginia Beach public school students in grades 2 through 5, and 8 percent of Portsmouth public school children in those grades, took ADHD medication last year — almost twice the national average.

According to this news story, 17% of white males in Portsmouth and Virginia Beach are receiving medication for ADHD at school.

But, can we really believe that your child and millions of other American children are suffering from a Ritalin deficiency?

Recent Scientific Studies Show that Foods and Other Dietary Ingredients Are Common Causes of ADHD

THE LANCET

"Seventy-six children were treated with a few-foods diet. Sixty-two improved and a normal range of behavior was achieved in 21. Other symptoms such as headache, abdominal pain and fits also improved.

". . . Twenty eight of the children completed a double-blind, crossover, placebo-controlled trial . . . "

J. Egger, et al, "Controlled Trial of Oligoantigenic Treatment in the Hyperkinetic Syndrome." *The Lancet*, 1985; ii 540-545.

"Nineteen of twenty-six children with ADHD (73%) responded favorably to an elimination diet. A double-blind, placebo-controlled food challenge was completed in 16 children."

M. Boris, and F. S. Mandel, "Food and Additives Are Common Causes of the Attention Deficit/Hyperactive Disorder in Children." *Annals of Allergy*, 1994; 72:462-467

"The results of a crossover trial on 19 children showed a significant effect for the provoking foods to worsen ratings of behavior and to impair psychological test performance. This study shows that observations of change in behavior associated with diet made by parents . . . can be reproduced using double-blind methodology and objective assessments."

C.M. Carter, et al, "Effects of a Few-Food Diet in Attention Deficit Disorder." *Archives of Diseases of Children*, 1993; 69:564-568.

THE JOURNAL OF PEDIATRICS

"A 21 day-double-blind, placebo-controlled study showed that behavioral changes and irritability, restlessness and sleep disturbances are associated with the induction of Tartrazine in some children."

K. S. Rowe and K. J. Rowe, "Synthetic Food Coloring and Behaviors: A Dose Response Effect in a Double-Blind, Placebo-Controlled, Repeated Measure Study" *Journal of Pediatrics* 1994; 125:691-698.

Your Child's ADHD May Be "Yeast-Connected."

In 1987, researchers at the University of Colorado and Yeshiva University studied a group of children who were being evaluated for school failure. *Those receiving medication for hyperactivity gave a history of greater than 10 ear infections.*

By comparison, only 20% of non-hyperactive children had more than 10 infections. (You'll find a a discussion of possible reasons on pages 62-69 of this book.)

Then, in July 1995, William Shaw, Ph.D., and colleagues of the Children's Mercy Hospital and the University of Missouri School of Medicine, Kansas City reported finding fungal metabolites in the urine of autistic children. They also noted a reduction in these metabolites and improvement of these children following therapy with antifungal drugs.

In his continuing research, Shaw studied the urine of 35 children with ADHD. He found elevated fungal metabolites in 25 of these children. Almost all gave a history of taking repeated courses of antibiotic drugs for ear and other infections.

Most of the children with elevated fungal metabolites studied by Shaw improved following treatment with nystatin, Diflucan and/or other antifungal medications and dietary changes.

Further information about Shaw's studies can be obtained from:
William Shaw, Ph.D., The Great Plains Laboratory, 9335 W. 75th Street, Overland Park, KS 66204. Ph. 913-341-8949. Fax: 913-341-6207. E-Mail:WilliamSha:@aol.com

Read what other professionals are saying . . .

"*Help for the Hyperactive Child* is an excellent guide for parents and teachers of hyperactive children. Indeed, much of the material is guidance for the parents of any child. The simple, concise presentation, plus the illustrations make for easy reading and sound instruction."

> George M. Wheatley, M.D.
> Past President, American Academy of Pediatrics
> Locust Valley, New York

"From my own clinical experience, I am certain that components of the diet play a major role in triggering disturbances of behavior in most children with the Attention Deficit Disorder with or without hyperactivity. . . . Dietary management is always to be preferred to medication."

> John W. Gerrard, D.M. (Oxon) F.R.C.P. (L), F.R.C.P. (C)
> Professor of Pediatrics (Emeritus)
> University of Saskatchewan
> Saskatoon, Saskatchewan

"I frequently observe a definite relationship between eating certain foods and hyperactivity, inability to attend school and academic performance. . . . At times results from dietary intervention are remarkable. Dr. Crook's new book will provide parents and professionals with timely, authoritative and helpful information."

> Douglas H. Sandberg, M.D.
> Professor of Pediatrics
> University of Miami
> Miami, Florida

"Dr. 'Billy' Crook is one in a million. Wouldn't it be wonderful to have a Dr. Crook in every town in the USA, dispensing the warm, thoughtful, helpful advice, based on many years of experience for which he is famous? Not every Mom can consult Dr. Crook personally, but every Mom *can* benefit from this clear, easy-to-understand book.

"This book should be required reading not only for all mothers of 'problem' children, but for doctors as well. Dr. Crook shows how to clear up hyperactivity, learning disabilities and other problems by diet and nutrition. . . . Without resort, in most cases, to those best-to-be-avoided drugs."

> Bernard Rimland, Ph.D.
> Founder, Autism Society of America
> Director, Institute for Child Behavior Research
> San Diego, California

HELP FOR THE
HYPERACTIVE CHILD

A practical guide offering parents
of ADHD children alternatives to

RITALIN

DESERT FOOTHILLS LIBRARY
PO BOX 4070
CAVE CREEK, AZ 85327

William G. Crook, M.D.
Illustrations by Cynthia Crook

PROFESSIONAL BOOKS
Jackson, Tennessee 38305

This book is dedicated to the millions of children with ADHD and their parents, grandparents and teachers.

The information in this book is intended to be helpful and educational. It is not intended to replace medical treatment or diagnosis. If the need be warranted, the reader should consult a health professional.

© 1991, 1997 William G. Crook, M.D.
Illustrations © 1991 Cynthia Crook

All rights reserved. Written permission must be secured from the publisher to use or reproduce any part of this book, except for brief quotations used in critical reviews or articles.

Published by Professional Books, Inc., 45 Conrad Drive, Jackson, Tennessee 38305, (901) 660-5027.

Book Design and Typography by ProtoType Graphics, Inc., Nashville, Tennessee.

Cover Design by Cynthia Crook, Nashville, Tennessee.

Library of Congress Cataloging-in-Publication Data

Crook, William Grant, 1917–
    Help for the Hyperactive Child

    Includes index.
    1. Behavioral and Learning Disorders in Children—Nutritional aspects.
    2. Attention Deficit Hyperactivity Disorder.
    3. Food Hypersensitivity—in infancy and childhood.
    91-06269
    ISBN   0-933478-18-6

Manufactured in the United States of America
4 5 6 7 8 9 10 — 00 99 98 97

Contents

Acknowledgments

If I listed all the people who've helped me and all the sources I've learned from, the bibliography of this book would be massive and the names legion.

Many colleagues will come across their ideas on these pages. As they do, they'll know how grateful I am for sharing them with me.

I'm indebted to Jean Smith, R.N., for her research, knowledge and practical experience in selecting and preparing "child-tested" foods which are nutritious, accepted—*and liked* by her four children. Credit is due Jean for all of the shopping tips, menus and other suggestions for parents (and others) responsible for feeding children and their families.

As with my other publications, I appreciate the charming artwork of my daughter Cynthia, who helps make what I write "come alive." Again I thank John Adams and the entire staff at ProtoType Graphics, Inc., Nashville, Tennessee, for their skillful production services.

Special words of appreciation are due Ken Keim, Nell Sellers, Janet Gregory, Sylvia Henson, Kay Ferree, Tara Mitchell and Brenda Harris. Ken edited the manuscript and coordinated the work of many people. Nell tested and evaluated the recipes and sources, Janet typed the manuscript and Brenda helped keep everyone else on track.

Foreword to the Fourth Printing

Since this book was first published in 1991, many people are becoming concerned about Ritalin. Here are excerpts from a June 8, 1997 syndicated article about this prescription medication by Scripps Howard News Service reporter, John Lang (published in the *Nashville Tennessean*):

> Americans would be horrified to learn that 2 million children across this nation are being given cocaine by their parents and doctors to make them behave better in school.
>
> It's so close to the truth that it takes a chemist to tell the difference. The effect is virtually the same. The kids are wired . . . What the drug does is make kids who have been bouncing off the walls and talking incessantly begin to sit still. They listen. They focus. Most make better grades.
>
> The drug is methylphenidate—or Ritalin by its most popular brand name—and it's a lucrative market for pharmaceutical companies in the United States. It can also mean big money for school systems that claim disabled students, and for some parents who claim disabled kids.

Lang also quoted Gene Haislip, recently retired deputy assistant administrator of the federal Drug Enforcement Administration (DEA) who said:

> We have become the only country in the world where children are prescribed such a vast quantity of stimulants that share virtually the same properties of cocaine.

According to the DEA, prescriptions for Ritalin have increased 600% during this decade. Most of the kids who are taking Ritalin are white, and from middle and upper class families. At school they line up at nurses' stations or principal's' offices to take their pills. Lang went on to say:

> This is a phenomenon seen nowhere else on Earth. The United States consumes five times more of this drug than all the rest of the world combined.

WHY THE NUMBERS OF CHILDREN WITH ADHD HAVE INCREASED

Nutritionally Deficient Diets

The quality of children's diet has steadily declined during the past 50 to 75 years. In the first half of the 20th century, the average family ate most of their meals at home. Included were a variety of foods, such as fruits, vegetables, cereal grains, meats and eggs.

By contrast, today few families sit down for the traditional family meal. Most families eat on the run and fill up on fast foods. Their intake of soft drinks has increased and these beverages are often loaded with sugar, food colorings and additives. So are most packaged and processed foods found on the shelves of supermarkets and convenience stores. In addition, many of these foods contain partially hydrogenated fats and oils.

Children who feast on these foods and beverages obtain inadequate amounts of vitamins and minerals. Their diets are also deficient in the essential fatty acids* found in fish oils, flax seeds, walnuts and other plant foods.

There are also dozens of other important nutrients called "phytopharmaceuticals" which are found in fruits and vegetables. These substances play an important role in keeping the brain and other parts of our bodies healthy and functioning properly.

Not long ago I read that some 15% of children eat only one vegetable a day—*French fried potatoes!*

---

*According to Jeffrey Bland, Ph.D., until recently, most artificial formulas given to infants during the early months of life, lacked Omega-3 essential fatty acids. He said that a deficiency of this important nutrient could contribute to health problems seen in children, including ADHD.

Antibiotics

When I opened my pediatric office almost 50 years ago, my contemporaries and I thought that antibiotics were "wonder drugs." So did our patients. Antibiotics enabled physicians to save the lives of many children suffering with meningitis, pneumonia and other formerly devastating infections.

It didn't take us many years to realize that these drugs were ineffective against viral infections and we nearly always resisted the request of parents who came in asking for an antibiotic for a mild respiratory infection.

But when a child came in with an earache, especially if he had fever, and an examination showed that the ear looked "red," we'd nearly always prescribe an antibiotic and the child usually improved. We felt that our antibiotic prescription was justified and helpful.

But gradually, during the late 1970s and early 80s, I began to wonder if repeated antibiotics for *all* ear infections were necessary. In a letter to the editor published in the July 1985 issue of *Pediatrics,* I said,

> I'm writing to point out ... that broad spectrum antibiotic drugs (including those commonly used in children to treat ear infections) cause alterations in the flora of the gastrointestinal tract, leading the overcolonization of *Candida albicans.* This organism, generally considered to be benign, has been shown . . . to produce both high and low molecular weight toxins.
>
> Clinical reports suggest that such candida toxins may cause wide systemic and nervous system symptoms, including immune system changes which may reduce the child's resistance and lead to a vicious cycle of infections.

In 1987, Randi J. Hagerman, M.D., and Alice R. Falkenstein, M.A., M.S.W. of the University of Colorado, and Yeshiva University published a study describing an association between recurrent otitis media in infancy and later hyperactivity (see page 62).

Since 1991 I've received reports from both parents and professionals which indicate that children who took repeated antibiotics for ear infections were much more apt to develop neurological problems, including ADHD, pervasive developmental disorders and autism.

Indoor Air Pollution

The air children breathe in their homes and schools includes chemicals of many types. Here are some of them: carpets, glues, laundry chemicals, cosmetics, formaldehyde, bathroom chemicals, insecticides and tobacco smoke. Two recent books provide a comprehensive discussion of these indoor pollutants which make many children and adults sick. Here's information about them.

One by Lynn Lawson, *Staying Well In A Toxic World* is authoritative, carefully documented and as readable as a paperback novel. To obtain a copy send a check for $18.95 to Lynn Lawson, P.O. Box 1732, Evanston, IL 60201.

Is This Your Child's World?—How You Fix The Schools and Homes That are Making Your Children Sick, is an equally informative book by Doris Rapp. You'll find this book in bookstores and health food stores throughout North America.*

Television

Most people, including my children and grandchildren enjoy TV. Yet studies today show that our children are spending more time looking at TV than they're spending in school, playing outdoors, reading or doing chores.

Television plays a role in causing ADHD. Here are two of the main reasons:

- TV promotes nutritionally-deficient foods, especially those loaded with sugar, food coloring and additives.
- TV keeps children indoors rather than letting them expend their energies in normal outdoor activities.

Family Stress

Financial Factors   To make ends meet, both parents may work outside of their homes. So their children may not receive enough rocking, singing to, reading to and

---

*You'll find a further discussion of chemical pollutants on pages 40–41 and 123–127, and a reference to pesticides on pages 118–122.

the other one-on-one psychological nutrients they require. Grandparents who might provide some of this care may live a thousand miles away. Moreover, those who live nearby often have full-time jobs.

Divorce Recent statistics show that 50% of American marriages end in divorce and such divorce often occurs in families with young children. In spite of the cooperative efforts of parents, children of divorce are frequently troubled with emotional problems.

Mobility Americans are on the move. They change homes, they change jobs, they change parts of the country. Parents also travel because of their jobs and parents my be absent from home for days or weeks at a time.

WHY THERE'S BEEN A GREAT INCREASE IN THE USE OF RITALIN

Ritalin Helps Relieve Symptoms

This medication works. It's readily available. It might be compared to taking aspirin for a headache. When people develop headaches, they don't think about the causes, they simply want relief.

The Advocacy of Ritalin by Physicians

Because Ritalin relieves symptoms most physicians recommend it and prescribe it. Here are two of the reasons:

- They are unaware of the double-blind, placebo-controlled studies which document the role food sensitivities (and other dietary factors) contribute to ADHD (see pages iv and 106–107). In addition, getting a child to comply with dietary recommendations is difficult.
- They are unaware of the clinical reports and ongoing scientific studies which support the relationship of repeated antibiotics and resulting yeast overgrowth to neurological problems in children (see pages v and 170–174).

The Advocacy of Ritalin by CHADD

Children and Adults with Attention Deficit Disorders (CHADD), an organization co-founded by Harvey Parker, a Florida psychologist in 1987, has urged parents and physicians to "rely on Ritalin," educational and psychological therapy. They have ignored the relationship of diet.

In commenting on ADHD and CHADD, John Merrow (executive producer of a public television documentary) said that CHADD was asking members of Congress to support a petition that seeks to loosen the rules governing the prescription of Ritalin.

In their petition, CHADD leaders said, "Ritalin is a beneficial and relatively benign medication which assists millions of children and is not dangerous or addictive."

But what CHADD *did not* disclose, Merrow said, is that it has been supported since 1988 by Ciga-Geigy, *the manufacturer of Ritalin!* Receiving nearly $900,000 in cash grants, along with in-kind services, CHADD has grown from a regional organization with a few hundred members into a national powerhouse with 35,000 members, 650 chapters and real clout in Washington.

COMMENTS ON THE DIET/BRAIN CONNECTION

During the past 75 years, numerous reports in the medical literature describe the relationship of food allergies to brain dysfunction (see pages 133–142). Yet, most physicians have remained skeptical. Heres why:

- Other studies which concluded that dietary changes played little, if any, role in causing ADHD (some of these negative studies were funded by the Sugar Association and other food industries).
- Most food sensitivities cannot be identified by the traditional allergy prick test.

I'm happy to report that since 1985, double-blind, placebo-controlled studies published in the peer-reviewed literature provide documentation for the relationship of food allergies to ADHD (see pages iv and 106–107).

A Special Message to
Parents, Grandparents and Teachers

This book is written for the parents and teachers of children with ADHD—especially those who

- give a history of colic, respiratory, digestive or skin disorders during the first year of life
- give a history of taking repeated or prolonged courses of antibiotic drugs for ear infections
- are bothered by allergies, including adverse reactions to foods and environmental chemicals
- give a history of craving sugar and eating a nutritionally deficient diet

It is written to provide help for these children without the use of Ritalin and/or other similar drugs. Although medications can help many hyperactive children "settle down" and concentrate, *the long term outlook for ADHD children who receive drug treatment only is dismal.*

Where I'm coming from: I'm a board-certified pediatrician, a Fellow of the American Academy of Pediatrics, the American College of Allergy and Immunology and the American Academy of Environmental Medicine.

When I entered pediatric practice in 1949 I knew nothing about the nutritional, biological, allergic, environmen-

tal, toxic and other factors which play an important part in causing ADHD and related behavior and learning problems in children.

In the mid-1950s I learned for the first time that sensitivities to common foods such as milk, chocolate, wheat and corn could adversely affect a child's nervous system.

In the late sixties and early seventies I learned that other dietary factors, including sugar and food colors, triggered nervous symptoms in many of my patients.

I also began to learn more about nutrition, including the important role that zinc, magnesium, calcium, the B vitamins and other nutrients contribute to normal behavior and learning.

Also, about the same time I learned that environmental toxins, including lead, mercury, insecticides and other chemicals, could affect a child's nervous system.

Then in 1979, I learned for the first time that repeated or prolonged courses of antibiotics could cause an imbalance of normal bacteria in the intestinal tract. This imbalance led to an overgrowth of the common and usually benign yeast *Candida albicans*.

I also learned that this yeast could put out toxins which adversely affect the immune system and the nervous system. Yeast-related health problems which then developed included repeated bouts of ear infections and nervous-system disorders, especially irritability, short attention span, inability to concentrate and hyperactivity.

I've described my findings and experiences in articles and commentaries in the medical and lay literature, and in my books including *The Yeast Connection Cookbook, The Yeast Connection and the Woman,* and *The Yeast Connection Handbook.*

This book summarizes my observations and provides

you with easy-to-follow instructions. It is designed to help you help your ADHD child sit still, pay attention and get along better at home, at school and in the neighborhood— *without the use of Ritalin or other stimulant medication.*

In my experience, such a program will help over 75% of children with ADHD so that they do not require stimulant medication.

A Special Message to

Physicians, Educators, Psychologists and Other Professionals

Ritalin helps many children "settle down" and perform better in school. I've prescribed it for a number of my patients during the past 20 years. I agree with the physicians who say, "If this medication is appropriately prescribed, and carefully monitored, serious and/or dangerous side effects rarely occur.

BUT...

I've found that Ritalin and/or other related medicines (including Cylert, Benzedrine, Dexedrine, Tofranil, Tegretol and Mellaril) are rarely needed if and when ...

1. The child is given a better diet—less sugar and "junk food," including processed and packaged foods which contain colors, flavors and additives. (Such foods are usually deficient in essential nutrients, such as vitamins, minerals and Omega 3 and Omega 6 fatty acids.)

2. The environment is "cleaned up." This means avoiding tobacco smoke, formaldehyde, insecticides, lead, cadmium and other toxic environmental substances.

3. Foods the child is sensitive to are identified using a carefully designed elimination diet. Following identification, such foods are avoided or consumed infrequently.

4. Anticandida therapy is prescribed for the child who gives a history of repeated or prolonged courses of antibiotic drugs for ear and/or other infections.

5. The child's psychological needs are appropriately managed so that his self-confidence and self-esteem increase.

6. A consistent program of management and discipline is established. This includes setting limits and making reasonable rules.

7. His educational needs are taken care of. This may include one-on-one tutoring and appropriate placement in school.

8. He is given nutritional supplements, including B Complex vitamins, magnesium, calcium, zinc, selenium and the essential fatty acids.

What You'll Find In This Book

Whether you are a parent, grandparent, teacher or sitter, helping the child with ADHD is a challenging and often frustrating responsibility which is often so difficult that you may become 'irritable and exhausted.

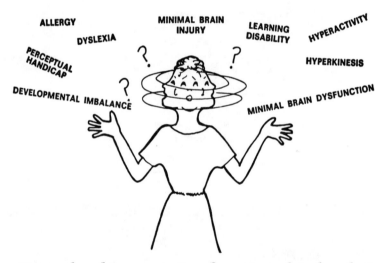

To make things easier for you, this book is divided into three sections. Each section deals with similar topics. You can look at and read everything in Section I, *An Overview,* in a few minutes. In this section, I make suggestions for cleaning up your child's diet.

In place of using beverages of poor nutritional quality, you'll find practical and easy to follow suggestions (including menus for breakfast, school lunches, main meals, snacks and beverages). Quite often when your ADHD child consumes better food he will improve.

I then suggest cleaning up your child's environment

and making lifestyle changes. You'll also find information about television so that you can control it rather than have it dominate your child's life. If your child is taking Ritalin, see if you can discontinue it, but return to your personal physician and ask for his help.

Because food allergies play an important role in causing ADHD, I provide you with easy-to-follow instructions for carrying out elimination/challenge diets. Then I discuss the child who has experienced repeated ear infections. Antibiotics which are customarily used in treating these ear problems lead to an overgrowth of the common yeast, *Candida albicans,* in the gut. Instructions are provided for coping with this problem.

I also make suggestions for discipline and management providing your child with emotional support and helping the child who is not doing well in school. Finally, I make suggestions about vitamins, minerals and other nutritional supplements.

In Section II, you will find more information about all of the topics covered in Section I. In this section you'll read about three children who improved following the comprehensive program described in this book.

Then I review my experiences during the past 35 years in treating children with food allergies and ADHD. I also include brief reviews of reports of others who have made similar observations.

I discuss Ritalin and the possible indications for its use. I point out that it does help control symptoms in many children with ADHD. Yet, *long term follow-up shows that the prognosis of the child with ADHD who receives drug treatment is dismal.*

Featured in this section of the book are illustrated menu suggestions to help you carry out an elimination diet. You will also find suggestions for helping your child stay on his diet without complaining or cheating.

In this section, you'll find additional information on yeast-related disorders and suggestions on discipline, management, psychological support, school readiness and nutritional supplements.

In Section III, *Still More Information,* you'll find Jean Smith's *Helpful Hints and Recipe Ideas for "Cleaning Up" the Diet.* This section also includes detailed questions and answers on the following subjects:

Feeding Your Child—Without Going Crazy,
Elimination Diets and
The Yeast Connection.

Section I
Overview

Introduction

Here's one mother's story: My son, Tom (not his name), used to be bothered by severe hyperactivity. Several specialists predicted he would experience severe learning disabilities and always need LD classes. When Tom was 4, a pediatric neurologist at a university medical center prescribed Ritalin. Yet, it didn't help. Moreover, it turned Tom into a "zombie."

In desperation we looked for other options. Working with a nutritionally oriented physician, we discovered that Tom suffered from numerous food sensitivities that "turned him on." We later learned that he also lacked several important nutrients.

Helping Tom wasn't easy. We had our ups and downs. Yet, we persisted and Tom graduated from high school in May 1989! Not only was he *not* hyperactive or learning disabled, he earned all A's during his high school career and was the class salutatorian. He scored 1400 on his SAT's, including a perfect 800 in Math, and is now attending business school at a major eastern university. At home, he's a joy to have around.

Our child is a real terror—so "hyper." Some days he just "bounces off the walls." We're concerned. Yet, we'd like to find help without using drugs. Is this possible?

You bet. Many hyperactive and inattentive children show remarkable improvement with no drugs at all.

We're excited! Please tell us more!

Most hyperactive and
inattentive children are
bothered by:

Food sensitivities
and
Nutritional deficiencies

And many give a history of repeated ear, throat, sinus, chest and other infections.

How are they related to hyperactivity?

Infections are treated
with antibiotic drugs.
These drugs encourage the
growth of the common
yeast, *Candida albicans*.

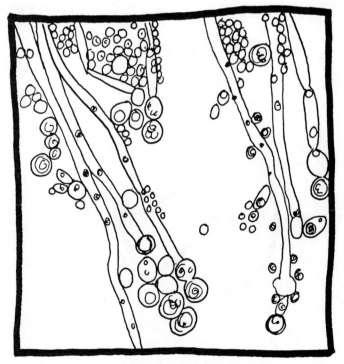

Microscopic view of yeasts

How can Candida yeasts be related to our child's problems?

Candida (like many other tiny organisms) puts out toxins (or poisons).

These toxins:
1. Weaken the immune system.
2. Irritate the nervous system.

Candida overgrowth also disturbs the mucous membranes of the gut.

○ - Normal Gut Flora

Y - *Candida albicans*

◖ - Pathogenic Bacteria

T - Toxins and/or Food antigens

INCREASED INTESTINAL CANDIDA

GREATER PERMEABILITY OF INTESTINAL MEMBRANE

INCREASED ABSORPTION OF TOXINS AND/OR FOOD ALLERGENS

As a result toxins and food allergens penetrate these membranes and go to other parts of the body.

What you're saying
is interesting—
yet our heads
are spinning.
Where and how
can we obtain
more information?

Read and study everything in this book.
Also read other publications including:

- *Alternative Medicine: The Definitive Guide* by the Burton Goldberg Group—Future Medicine Publishing Inc., 1994
- *Back to Health: Yeast Control* by Dennis Remington and Barbara Higa, Vitality House International, 1989
- *Candida-Related Complex—What Your Doctor Might Be Missing* by Christine Winderlin with Keith Sehnert, 1996, Taylor Publishing Company, 1550 West Mockingbird Lane, Dallas, TX 75235
- *Dr. Braly's Food Allergy & Nutrition Revolution* by James Braly, Keats Publishing Company, New Canaan, Connecticut, 1992
- *Encyclopedia of Nutritional Supplements* by Michael Murray, Keats Publishing Company, New Canaan Connecticut, 1996
- *Feeding the Brain—How Foods Affect Children* by Keith Conners, Plenum Press, New York and London, 1990
- *Healing Childhood Ear Infections*—Revised, North Atlantic Books, Berkley, CA, Michael Schmidt, 1996
- *Is This Your Child? Discovering and Treating Unrecognized Allergies* by Doris Rapp, William Morrow and Company, 1992
- *No More Ritalin—Treating ADHD Without Drugs* by Mary Ann Block, Kensington Books, 1996
- *Reclaiming Our Health* by John Robbins, H. J. Kramer, Inc., P.O. Box 1082, Tiburon, CA 94920, 1996
- *Staying Well in a Toxic World* by Lynn Lawson, Noble Press, 1993
- *Super-Immunity for Kids* by Leo Galland and Dian Buchman, Dutton, NY, 1988
- *The Missing Diagnosis* by Orian Truss, 2614 Highland Avenue, Birmingham, AL 35205
- *The Myth of the ADD Child* by Thomas Armstrong, Dutton, NY, 1996
- *Why Can't My Child Behave?* by Jane Hersey, Pear Tree Press, P.O. Box 30146, Alexandria, VA 22310
- *The Yeast Connection Handbook* by William Crook, Professional Books, 1996/1997
- *The Yeast Connection Cookbook* by William Crook, Professional Books, 1989

Why do we need to read and study?

The more you know, the better. Your child with hyperactivity resembles an overloaded camel.

As you remove bundles of straw, other health problems* will also improve.

---

*Fatigue, irritability, headache, ear infections, allergic rhinitis, asthma and other chronic complaints.

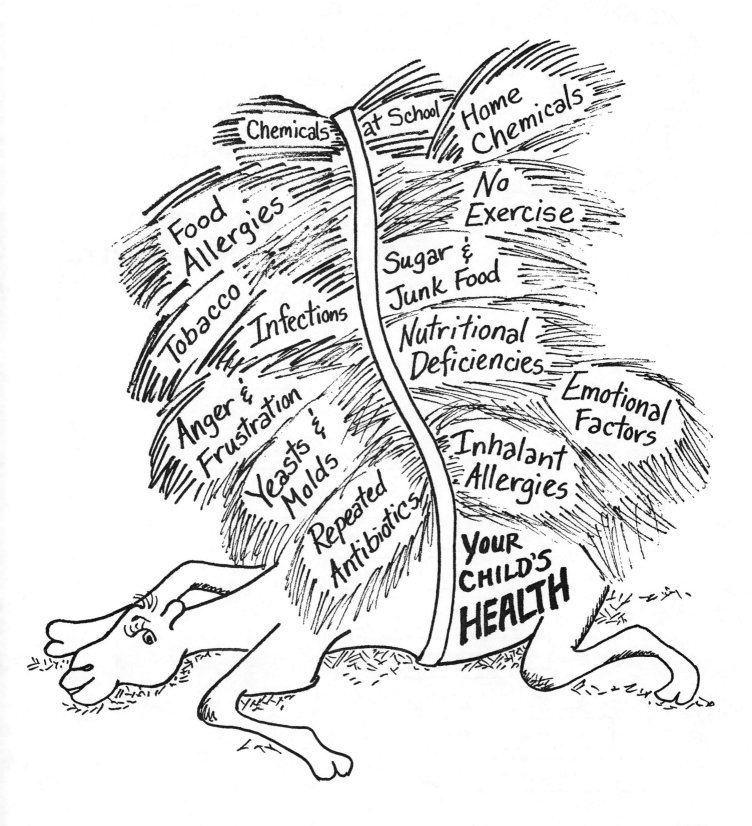

We'll do this reading and studying as soon as possible—but we're eager to help our child *now*. What do we do first?

As a first step, clean up your child's diet and get rid of junk foods.

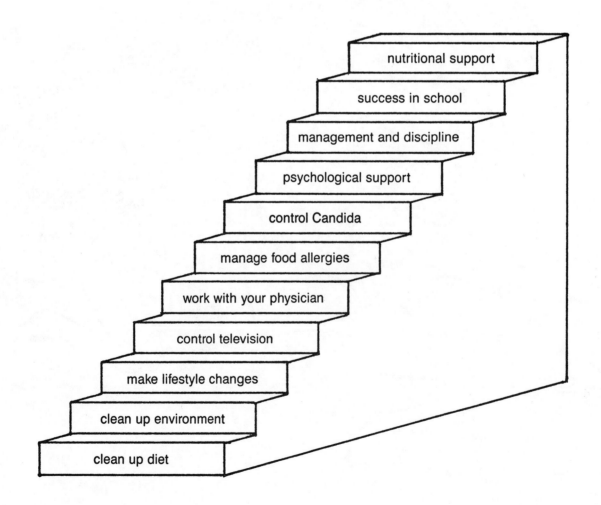

- nutritional support
- success in school
- management and discipline
- psychological support
- control Candida
- manage food allergies
- work with your physician
- control television
- make lifestyle changes
- clean up environment
- clean up diet

Clean Up the Diet

The diet of Americans during the last several decades has changed dramatically since pioneer days. We live in a "fast-food" society and eat processed and packaged foods which contain sugar, food coloring, flavors, chemicals, additives and pesticides. We drink beverages that are loaded with sugar, phosphates, caffeine, food colors, aspartame and other additives.

Changing your child's diet won't be easy, yet, many hyperactive/inattentive children will improve significantly—even dramatically—when you make changes suggested on the next few pages.

Cut down—better still avoid—
Foods and drinks containing sugar . . .

And those containing food colors, phosphates, aspartame and other additives and flavors.

Processed and packaged foods containing the "bad fats"—coconut oil, palm oil, other and/or hydrogenated or partially hydrogenated vegetable oils.

Offer more . . .

potatoes, peas, beans, sweet
potatoes, tomatoes, carrots,
onions and celery.

Also try some other vegetables:
asparagus, beets, broccoli,
brussels sprouts, cabbage,
cauliflower, eggplant,
kale, jicama, peppers,
radishes, snow peas,
squash and turnips.

Offer more . . .

Fruits

Whole Grains

Fish *

*Choose those low in fat. Cod, haddock, flounder, grouper, pollock, snapper and tuna are relatively safe *if* caught offshore.

Buy special vegetable oils*

Diversify your child's diet with grain alternatives.

*Organically grown, unrefined or "expeller pressed." Available in health food stores and in some supermarkets.

Look for chemically uncontaminated foods.

Become label-conscious and join others who are working for safer foods.

Become an informed consumer. Read:

Ingredients—Label Reading

LABELS DON'T TELL THE ENTIRE STORY

Facts

1. Ingredients are listed by weight in descending order.
2. Some ingredients may not be listed by specific names (i.e., flavorings, color, spices, cultures, enzymes, etc.).
3. Other ingredients (including waxes and other chemicals may *not* be listed at all).
4. Fat percentages (i.e., 80% fat-free) are based on weight, not calories.

Beware of "Catch Phrases" on labels—read ingredients.

Look for

1. Minimally processed foods
2. Low sugar; or fruit-or fruit-juice-sweetened items to be used in limited amounts
3. Low fat; and NO saturated or hydrogenated oils

Avoid or Limit

1. Highly processed foods
2. Saturated oils and fats and tropical oils (palm & coconut)
3. Hydrogenated oils
4. Partially hydrogenated oils (when possible)
5. Food dyes and colorings*
6. Many chemicals and preservatives
7. Artificial sweeteners, including NutraSweet®

More About Sugar and Other Sweeteners

1. Should be listed toward the last in the list of ingredients
2. A product may contain more than one kind of sugar.
3. Choose naturally occurring sweets over refined/processed sweets.

Naturally occurring sweetners:	Less processed:	More refined:
1. Juice, fruit juice, fruit juice concentrate	date sugar	sugar
	Sucanet	beet sugar
	brown rice syrup	fructose
	almond syrup	sorbitol
2. Honey	ribbon cane sugar	mannitol
3. Maple syrup	malted barley	xylitol
4. Aguamiel**		dextrose
5. Stevia rebaudiana***		maltodextrose
		glucose
		sucrose
		corn syrup
		corn fructose

---

*Annato is a natural occurring substance that seems to be a safe food coloring.
**Aguamiel is a natural sweetener from cactus plants available in health food stores.
***A herbal sweetner available from Allergy Resources, 1-800-873-3529.

Good Foods for Your Child

Breakfast Suggestions:

Multigrain pancakes or waffles

Whole wheat toast

"All fruit" spreads

Limited amounts of:

Maple syrup   Fruit syrup   Honey

Hearty muffins—may add fresh or dried fruits

Nuts

Acceptable cold cereals* with milk or juice. Add seasonal fruits, raisins or nuts (chopped if under age 4).

*Cereals which contain little or no sugar and no colors and additives include Nutri Grain, Cheerios, Grape Nuts plus many obtainable from health food stores.

Lean meats—thin sliced, minimally processed

Hot cereals—may add seasonal fruits or chopped nuts

Rice cakes or mini rice cakes

Pastry poppers*

Eggs occasionally. Boiled, poached, scrambled with proper oil.

Fresh fruits

Hard cheeses

Sliced potatoes or apples slightly sautéed

Banana nut, fruited breads

*Nature's Warehouse brand. These are free of sugar and hydrogenated fats.

Sample Menus:

Whole-grain pancakes or waffles with small amount of honey, syrup, fruit spreads

Grilled thin-sliced turkey or chicken

Grapefruit half, or sliced orange

Boiled egg sliced on whole-wheat or multigrain bread with cheese melted on it

Fresh fruit combination i.e., strawberries and banana or pineapple

Pastry poppers—(Nature's Warehouse)

Sliced apples or pears

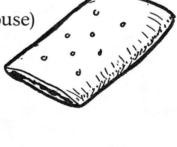

Milk or "acceptable" juice can be added to each breakfast

Quick—Fast:

1. Rice cake with nut butter and banana or fruit spread

2. Rice cake or whole-wheat toast with melted cheese

Thin, breakfast-style pork chops, or
other nonprocessed meats—grilled
or baked
Sliced potatoes
Apples—cooked or pan sautéed
Muffin or multigrain biscuits

Acceptable cold cereal* with or
without added seasonal fresh fruit,
raisins, nuts, etc.
Use milk or acceptable juice

Hot cereal (Quaker Oats, Cream
of Wheat or Rice, rice, quinoa,
millet, etc.)
Add fresh or dried fruits or nuts
sweetened with small amount of
honey, syrup or fruit spread.

Whole-wheat bagel with yogurt
cheese and fruit spread
Banana or peach
Milk or juice

---

*Nutri Grain, Cheerios, Grape Nuts, etc.

Lunch Suggestions:

Whole-grain muffin or bagel

Yogurt cheese mix

Sliced "unprocessed" meats

Nut butters*

Homemade soups

Nuts and acceptable trail mix

*Store upside down so most of the oil will settle at the bottom of jar.

Salads

Vegetable sticks

Fruits—fresh and individual juice packed cans or boxes

Grilled meat and vegetables

Less processed hard cheeses

Fruit or nut breads with or without yogurt cheese or fruit spread

Occasional or limited:

Fruit leather*

Juice-sweetened cookies

*Stretch Island and Knudsen are two brands which are pure fruit and contain no artificial colors, flavors or preservatives.

School Lunch Ideas:

Pita or pocket bread filled with:

1. Tuna salad

2. Egg salad

3. Chunks of turkey, chicken, beef, port or salmon

Top with tomato slices or chunks, pickles, grated "hard" cheeses, sprouts, grated carrots

Acceptable whole-grain breads, muffins, biscuits or rice cakes, with:

1. Sliced pork, beef, turkey, chicken, wild game, unprocessed meats—dressed with hard cheeses, lettuce, tomato, pickles

2. Yogurt cheese topped with cucumbers, watercress, spinach, lettuce varieties or kiwi

3. Yogurt cheeses mixed with olive, tuna, ground cooked meats with pickle relish, fruits or fruit spreads

4. Hard cheeses dressed with lettuce and/or sliced pineapple, drained and packed in separate sandwich bag

5. Nut butters with banana and/or fruit spread

Acceptable:
Chips or pretzels

1 or 2 juice-sweetened cookies

Fruit leather (Knudsen or Stretch Island)

Individual juice packed fruit or unsweetened applesauce

Vegetable sticks (i.e., carrots, celery, cucumbers, zucchini)

Fresh fruits—grapes, oranges, apples, pears, peaches, nectarines, plums, kiwi, etc. (Caution: Beware of pits and young children)

Raisins

Roasted peanut butter, almond butter or cashew butter with crackers

Trail mixes

Salads:

1. Lettuce varieties topped with chunks of unprocessed meats, grated cheeses and vegetables like carrots, celery, zucchini, Jerusalem artichoke, cucumbers, etc. Acceptable dressing.

2. Tuna or chicken grape and nut salad. (Can substitute apple for grape)

3. Low-fat cottage cheese and fruits with hearty muffin

At Home or Eating Out:

Grilled meat or fish
Baked potatoes or rice
Salad or spinach
Fresh fruit

Homemade soup
Cornbread
Sliced fruit

Main Meals:

Grilled, baked or broiled minimally processed meats or fish

Fresh (if possible) or fresh frozen steamed or baked vegetables

Raw vegetables and salads

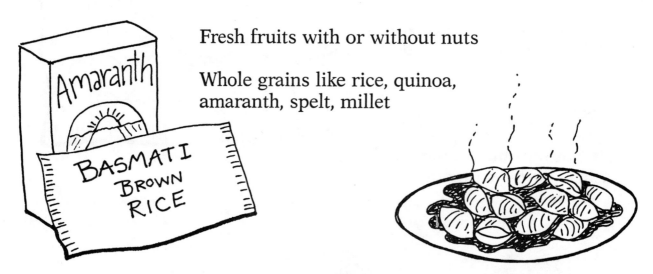

Fresh fruits with or without nuts

Whole grains like rice, quinoa, amaranth, spelt, millet

Whole-grain pastas, including spaghetti, noodles, spirals and elbows

Whole-grain breads, muffins, biscuits or rolls

Homemade soups

Sample Menus:

Grilled, baked or broiled meat—pork, beef, chicken, turkey, wild game or fish, with:

1. Baked potato or rice or sweet potato
   Green beans, peas or spinach
   Whole-grain biscuit or bread

2. Steamed carrots and broccoli

3. Broccoli or brussels sprouts, squash and onions

Homemade spaghetti (ground beef, turkey or chicken)

Vegetable salad
Whole-wheat French bread

Grilled hamburger or chicken breast on whole-wheat bun dressed with lettuce and tomato, baked beans or sautéed onions and potato slices, coleslaw

Thin-sliced meat and vegetable stir-fry served as is or over whole-grain noodles
Carrot and raisin (or pineapple) salad

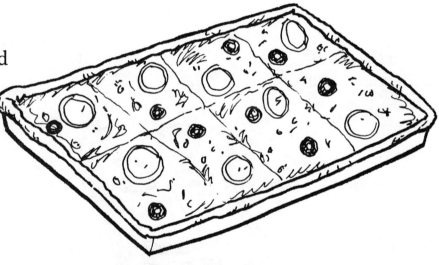

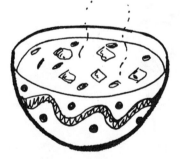

Homemade soup
Muffin
Cottage cheese and fruit

Homemade pizzas with whole grain crust or on whole grain French bread

Homemade tacos (using organic taco, or taco cooked in nonhydrogenated oil) or burritos
Salad and/or vegetable sticks with or without dip

Sweets, Snacks, and Sips:

Fresh Fruits:

Whole, sliced, combinations with or without flavored sauce, nuts or raisins

May be accompanied by nut or fruit breads, 1 or 2 juice-sweetened cookies

Baked fruit with crunchy topping

Homemade fruit cobbler (with low sugar)

Occasional:

Some types of frozen yogurt

Homemade bundt cakes, low in sugar and saturated fats

Homemade cookies, low in sugar and saturated fats

Yogurt "cream" cheese pies, topped with sliced fruit

Happy Faces:

Open sandwiches with nut butters or yogurt cheese. Make faces with fruit, vegetable pieces.

Ants on a Log:

Celery stuffed with nut butter or yogurt cheese topped with raisins or nut pieces

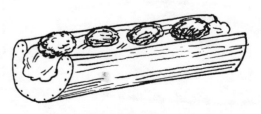

Cold Drinks:

Herbal teas with or without fruit juices

Spritzers (carbonated fruit juices—no additives)

Milk

Some acceptable fruit juices (better to eat the fruit)

Ice water—with or without lemon, lime or orange slices

Mineral or spring waters

Hot Drinks:

Apple juice or apple blends (100% juice), apple ciders

Tomato soup with crackers

Fun Drinks:

Made with blender or shaved or cracked ice

Frappés—fruit-juice concentrates, milk, ice, fruits

Slushes—ice, fresh fruit, and juice concentrates

Snacks:

Acceptable:

Popcorn
Cheese and crackers or muffins

Nut butters with bread, crackers

Muffins, fruit slices or vegetable
sticks

Nut butter and puffed cereal balls

Fresh fruit slices or pieces on a stick

Oven roasted or dry-roasted peanuts,
Hazel nuts, almonds, pecans, etc.
(chopped for young children)

Raisins and other dried fruits
(brush teeth afterward)

Trail mixes from above

Vegetable sticks

Bread sticks

Pretzels

Whole-grain "pizza" French bread

Dips:

Yogurt based

Nut butter based

Tomato based (salsas)

Clean Up Your Child's Environment

Everyone knows that chemical pollutants in the air, soil, food and water are adversely affecting us and our children. Yet, you may be surprised to learn that indoor air pollutants are bothering us more than those we're exposed to outdoors. You can help your child and other family members too—by cleaning up your home environment.

Chemicals your child is exposed to at school may also adversely affect your child. These include floor cleaners and waxes, chemical deodorants in bathrooms, insecticides, perfume, permanent markers and mimeograph paper.

Exposure to chemicals on the way to school may also affect him, including diesel fumes from idling buses, colognes and tobacco inside the bus or car.

Reduce home and school pollutants.

Make Lifestyle Changes

Life today is stressful—under the best of circumstances. And it's especially difficult for the parents of a hyperactive/inattentive child. As your child improves, things will get better for you.

Even though you can't do everything at once, don't feel guilty. Do the best you can.

Spend more quality time with your child.

Control Television

Television is a fantastic, modern-day "miracle." It's part of everyone's life. TV entertains, informs and educates us.

But according to Action for Children's Television, a nonprofit child advocacy organization, *American children watch, on the average, about 28 hours of television a week!!* So they're spending more time looking at TV than they're spending outdoors playing. They're even spending more time looking at TV than they're spending at school.

Along with many other observers, I'm concerned about the adverse effects of TV on children. Moreover, I feel that it contributes to the growing epidemic of hyperactivity and attention deficits in children.

In helping your hyperactive child you'll need to control television.

Control television? How does television contribute to hyperactivity?

Television may contribute to hyperactivity in several ways:

TV ads promote cereals and other nutritionally deficient foods containing sugar, food coloring and additives.

TV keeps children indoors.

Many TV programs encourage aggressive behavior.

TV interferes with studies, reading and family time.

It exposes children to more electromagnetic radiation.

Please give us suggestions for controlling TV.*

Don't let TV dominate your home.

Read to your child—play family games.

*See "More About Television" in Section II of this book and pages 32–34, 269–272, 303–304 in *Solving the Puzzle of Your Hard-to-Raise Child*.

Look at Saturday morning TV—especially the ads. Then substitute quality advertisement-free video tapes.

Don't put a TV set in your child's room.

Adverse Effects of Television

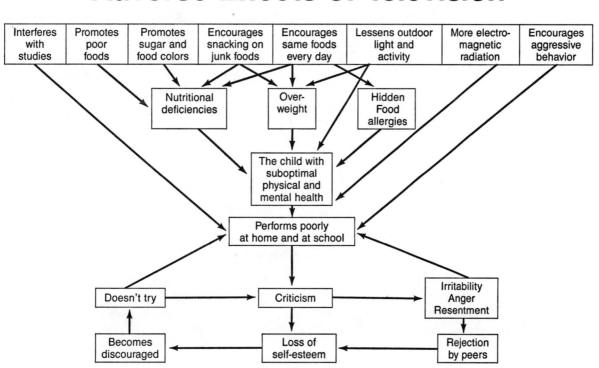

Work with Your Physician

During the 1980s, researchers in England and Canada found that hyperactivity and other nervous-system symptoms were often diet related. Two reports of their research findings were published in major pediatric journals in 1989 (see Section II).

An American allergist, Sami L. Bahna, M.D., Chairman of the Department of Allergy and Immunology at the Cleveland Clinic Foundation, has also observed that hyperkinesis may be a symptom of food allergy. A report in the April 1988 issue of *Consult,* published by the Cleveland Clinic Foundation, stated, *"The majority of food sensitive patients cannot be diagnosed through—routine tests. Dr. Bahna considers the elimination challenge test the Gold Standard for diagnosis."*

Because of these and other reports, many physicians have recently become interested in helping their hyperactive patients by changing their diets.

If your child is taking Ritalin—or even if he isn't—your task will be made easier by working with your physician.

Call and make an appoint-
ment with your physician.

Then take your child in for a
checkup and consultation.

If your child is taking Ritalin (or a related drug) tell your physician you'd like help in reducing the dose—or stopping it.

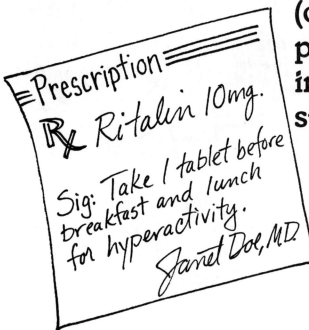

Then . . .
show your physician this book.

To obtain reprints of
five scientific studies which
document the relationship of
diet to ADHD write* to:

The International Health Foundation (IHF)
P.O. Box 3494
Jackson, TN 38303

*Please ask specifically for "reprints of scientific studies that document the relationship
of diet to ADHD" and send a mailing label and $10.00 to help with costs.

OK. You've done some of your "homework" and visited with your doctor. You've also "cleaned up" your child's diet and made "lifestyle changes."

We've worked at it!!!

You're ready now to "move ahead" and find out if your child is sensitive to something he's eating every day.

Track Down Hidden Food Allergies

Nervous system symptoms caused by food allergies* have been described by dozens of professionals during the past several decades. Yet, this relationship is often overlooked by physicians and other professionals. Here's why: *Most food allergies (and/or other adverse food reactions) cannot be determined by allergy skin tests or laboratory tests. Instead, they must be identified by a carefully designed, properly executed elimination diet.* Any dietary ingredient can provoke nervous symptoms, including milk, food colors, additives, sugar, wheat, corn, chocolate, yeast and citrus.

In this section you'll find easy-to-follow instructions for carrying out a trial diet. Such a diet will help you identify foods that contribute to your child's hyperactivity and other systemic and nervous symptoms.

---

*Four types of allergic reactions have been identified and classified. One of these (Type I) is mediated through a blood fraction called "IgE." Reactions of this type produce positive scratch tests in individuals sensitive to pollens and other inhalants, and much less commonly in individuals sensitive to food. However, *many and perhaps most individuals who show the adverse food reactions discussed in this book will not show positive scratch or other immunologic tests.*

At this time (1990), in spite of studies by many investigators during the past few years, many of the mechanisms and explanations for these food reactions remain obscure. Since they may not involve antigen and antibody reactions, many immunologists and other physicians prefer to call these food reactions "intolerances," "hypersensitivities," "adverse reactions," or "sensitivities." You'll find a further discussion in Section II.

How do we find out if our son's hyperactivity is caused by something he's eating?

You carry out an elimination diet* avoiding many of his favorite foods.

What will we look for?— How will we know he's allergic?

If he's sensitive to the foods he avoids, his symptoms will improve or disappear when the foods are eliminated. And they'll return when he eats them again.

*If your child has had asthma or experienced swelling or other serious allergic reactions, get the help and consultation of your physician before carrying out this diet.

What do we do first?

Discuss the diet with your child and other family members. Ask for their cooperation.

How long does it take to do the diet?

The elimination part of the diet lasts about a week—or until your child shows a convincing improvement in his symptoms.

Then, the second week, return the eliminated foods to his diet one food per day and see if his symptoms return.

Please tell us more about the diet.

Pick a convenient time. Don't try it during a holiday.

Send your child's lunch to school—discuss the diet with his teacher.

Begin a symptom and food diary 3 days before you start the diet.

Continue the diary while your child is eliminating foods and while he's eating them again.

Foods Your Child Can Eat or Drink

Any vegetable but corn and
any fruit but citrus.

Any meat but bacon,
sausage, hot dogs
and luncheon meat.

Oats, rice, barley, and the
grain alternatives, amaranth
quinoa and buckwheat.

Unprocessed nuts.

Water (preferably
bottled or filtered).

Foods He Should Avoid*

milk

soft drinks, Kool-Aid, punches

citrus

wheat

food colors, additives and flavors

processed and packaged foods*

corn

chocolate

sugar

yeast

*You'll find menu suggestions and other information about food allergies and elimination diets in Section II and III.

**These foods usually contain many "hidden" ingredients, including sugar, yeast, corn, milk, wheat, food colors, preservatives and flavors.

Suppose we identify several foods which trigger our child's hyperactivity—yet he continues to experience symptoms and they're caused by something he's eating.

You'll have to search further. Here are my suggestions:

1. Consider the possibility that chemical contaminants in or on your child's foods may be causing problems. *

2. Remember that any food can cause symptoms, including beef, chicken, pork, peanuts and other common foods.

*See Section II.

To identify sensitivity to these foods try the Caveman Diet* for a week.

On this diet your child avoids any and every food he eats more than once a week.

*You'll find more information about this diet in Section II.

Control Candida

Recent scientific studies show that children who experience repeated ear infections during the early years of life are much more apt to become hyperactive than other children. On the next few pages, you'll learn why these two troublesome problems which affect children may be related.*

An Association Between Recurrent Otitis Media in Infancy and Later Hyperactivity

Randi J. Hagerman, MD, Alice R. Falkenstein, MA, MSW

An association between the frequency of otitis media in early childhood and later hyperactivity is reported in this study. The subjects were 67 children referred to a child development clinic for evaluation of school failure. Ranging from 6 to 13 years old, all the children demonstrated specific school learning problems, and 27 were also considered hyperactive by two or more raters. Sixteen of the hyperactive children were treated with central nervous system stimulant medication. In retrospect, there was positive correlation between an increasing number of otitis media infections in early childhood and the prese... and severi... of hyperactive behavior. Ninety-four percent of childre... medicated ... hyperacti... ...d three ...ore otitis infections, and 69 percent had greater than 10 in... ...ons. In ...riso... ...rcen... ...-hyperac*... school-failure patients had three or more infe... ...d ... ...infe... Twenty-two of 28 children (79%) k... ...o have ... ...titis before 1 year of age.

O TITIS ... ... episode within the
fectious diseases of ... ...plicated by persistent
rative stud... ... ...t of children
of the children had a... ... ...d effusion at a 2-week
age and one third had ... ...dren with oti-
media.[1,2] Ingr... ... ...or weeks after an-
prospectively that half of 2,4...
sode of otitis and 18 perce... ... ...ion is ... ...s the most
sodes by 5 years of age. L... ge popula... ... ...ia and is responsible
shown that five to six percent of chi... ...ve ... 8 pe... ...t of children with
than 10 infections by 6 to 8 years ol... The gre... ... ...ns ha... ...avera... ...s of 10 dB or less; 92 per-
incidence of acute otitis media occurs between 6 ... cen... ...ave a he... ...ng loss bet...en 16 and 40 dB sec-
24 months of age. Recurrent episodes of otitis are as... ondary to the effusion.[7] The association between the

"69% of children being evaluated for school failure who were receiving medication for hyperactivity, gave a history of greater than 10 ear infections ... By comparison, only 20% of non-hyperactive children had more than 10 infections."

number of otitis media infections and the presence of persistent otitis media with effusion (OME) has been documented.[8] The risk of OME is seven times normal with two infections, eight times normal with three to six infections, and 165 times normal with more than six episodes of otitis media.

Recurrent OME and fluctuating hearing loss in early childhood have been associated with cognitive, language, and learning deficits in the school-age child.[9-21]

From the Child Development Unit, The Children's Hospital and Department of Pediatrics, University of Colorado, Health Sciences Center, Denver, Colorado and Yeshiva University, Psychology Department, New York, New York.

Funded in part by the Colorado Commission of Higher Education—CCHE—School Failure Grant #2-5-33997.

Correspondence to Randi J. Hagerman, MD, Child Development Unit, The Children's Hospital, 1056 East 19th Avenue, Denver, CO 80218.

Received for publication October 1985, revised December 1985 and June 1986, and accepted October 1986.

CLINICAL PEDIATRICS   May 1987

Used with permission.

*You'll find a further discussion in *The Yeast Connection Handbook*, pp. 71–79.

Repeated ear infections play a role in causing hyperactivity.

How and why could these two conditions be related?

When your child develops an ear infection . . .

he is treated with broad-spectrum antibiotic drugs.

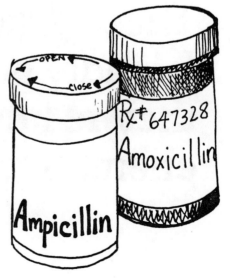

These drugs knock out friendly germs while they're knocking out enemies.

Candida yeasts aren't affected by antibiotics.

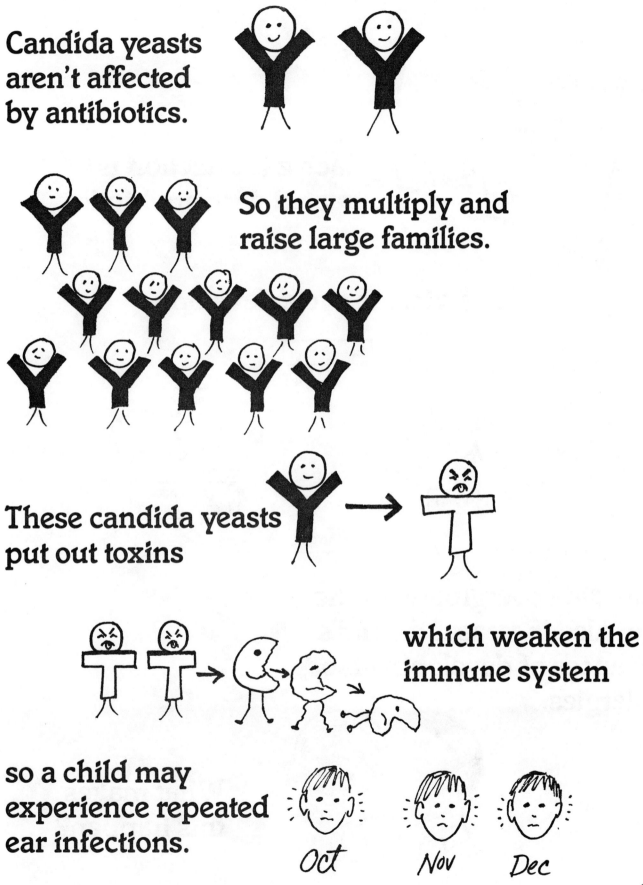

So they multiply and raise large families.

These candida yeasts put out toxins

which weaken the immune system

so a child may experience repeated ear infections.

Oct   Nov   Dec

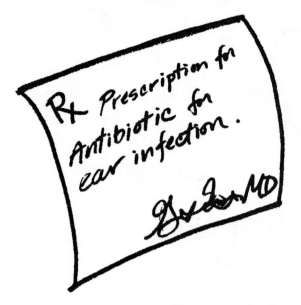

Each ear infection is treated with antibiotics.

So a vicious cycle develops.

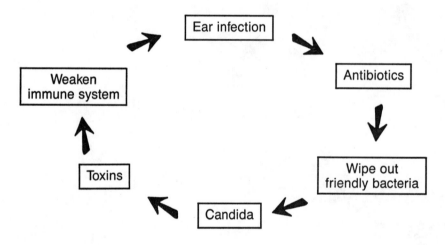

Ear infection → Antibiotics → Wipe out friendly bacteria → Candida → Toxins → Weaken immune system →

Candida overgrowth in the gut also increases a child's chances of developing food allergies.

What makes this happen?

Candida weakens the normal
intestinal membrane, creating
what has been termed as a
"leaky gut."

Toxins and food allergens
then pass through this
membrane and go to other
parts of the body.

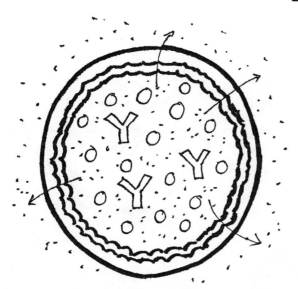

Normal intestine
(cross section)

"leaky gut"

Nutrients

Normal gut flora

Candida albicans

Toxins and/or
food allergens

Food allergens may cause nasal congestion, abdominal pain, and other symptoms. They may also affect your child's nervous system. *

Headache

Hyperactivity

Tired and sleepy

Irritability

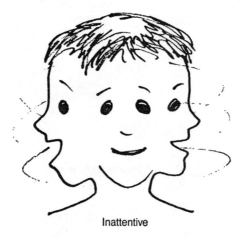

Inattentive

Spaced out

*Candida toxins may also affect your child's nervous system.

If our child's problems are candida related, what do you advise?

He should avoid foods that promote yeast growth— especially sugar . . .

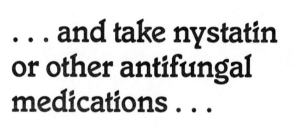

. . . and take nystatin or other antifungal medications . . .

. . . plus other substances that discourage yeast growth.

Psychological Support

Hyperactive children frustrate and annoy everyone around them. Their behavior understandably causes them to be criticized, punished and rejected.

I've found that most difficult, overactive children settle down and perform better within a few weeks (or even a few days!) after following the program described in this book. Then it's easier for parents to give them more of the "psychological vitamins" they desperately need.

The hyperactive, inattentive, impulsive child annoys his teachers and disrupts the class.

We realize this because he also irritates and frustrates us and his siblings.

And because of his un-pleasant behavior the hyperactive child is apt to be ignored, rejected, criticized or punished. So he suffers from a loss of self-esteem.

Yes, our son becomes frus-trated, irritable and angry . . . and at times depressed. Yet, like all children, he yearns for attention and recognition.

To gain this attention, many hyperactive children become "the class clown" or neighborhood bully who is caught up in a vicious cycle.

Vicious Cycles in a Hyperactive/Inattentive Child

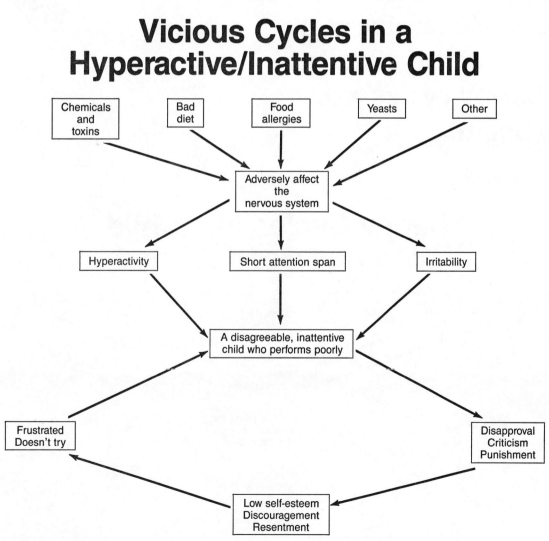

How can we break up this vicious cycle?

When you follow a comprehensive management program, your child will begin to improve. As he performs better, he'll receive more "psychological vitamins" and happy cycles will soon begin.

Happy Cycles in a Child Who Has Been Helped

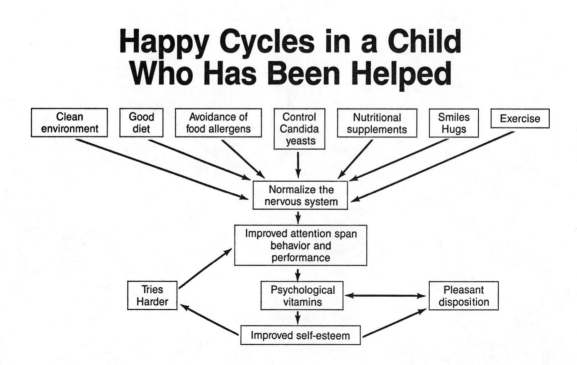

Tell us about these "psychological vitamins." Give us suggestions for administering them.

They're best given "one to one." They include smiles, praise, listening, touching, holding, hugging and approving.*

*See Section II and also pages 237–249 and 258 of *Solving the Puzzle of Your Hard-to-Raise Child*.

Management—and Discipline

In guiding and managing your child, you must take charge. You *are* an AUTHORITY. (An authority is one who knows more about a subject than the person he is dealing with!)

Know what to expect of your child. Make reasonable rules and set limits. But don't expect your child to live up to adult standards. Praise good behavior—and ignore minor "bad" behavior.

Discipline means teaching or training. Punishment, while sometimes necessary, is the least effective form of discipline.

Also, as pointed out elsewhere in this book, disagreeable, obnoxious and unacceptable behavior is often caused by nutritional, allergic and toxic reactions in the nervous system.

Right from birth our child was strong-willed and determined. And managing him became even more difficult when he developed hyperactivity and attention deficits. Do you believe in discipline?

Absolutely and positively. Discipline is essential. Yet, "discipline" does not mean punishment. Instead, it is teaching and training a child. Also, maintaining control.

Could you give us suggestions?

Take charge. Make reasonable rules and set limits you can successfully enforce.

Be consistent.

Notice (smile, pat, hug) and praise good behavior.

Ignore minor "bad behavior" (unless he's breaking rules or interfering with the rights of others).

How do you feel about punishment?

Punishment is the least effective form of discipline, yet it is sometimes necessary.

We agree. Could you give us suggestions?

Okay, here are a few of them:

Don't make too many rules.

Don't threaten or nag.

Disapprove of the act, but not of the child.

Avoid excessive explanations.

Be firm and concise.

Never bribe.

Suppose we *have* to punish?

The most effective punishment varies from one child to another.

Discipline in private.

Punishment must be immediate—and must fit the crime.

Try isolation for five minutes.

Don't spank in anger.

Never spank with more than one swat.

Remember, isolating, spanking, or other punishment is never as effective as rewarding his behavior.

Is there anything else we need to know?

Yes. Few children want to be "bad." Look for and find the causes of his objectionable behavior, rather than treating the symptom.*

*See more about Management and Discipline in Section II.

Helping Your Child Succeed in School

Most children with hyperactivity and attention deficits experience trouble learning to read and keeping up in school. In this section you'll find suggestions which have helped many children.

Many hyperactive children develop learning problems.

That's the situation with our son and he's having trouble keeping up.

I'm not surprised. And when children fall behind their classmates, their self-esteem falls and they often become depressed.

Our son *is* depressed and so discouraged he's stopped trying. Would repeating the first grade help?*

*Get a copy of *Is Your Child in the Wrong Grade in School?* by Louise Bates Ames, from your public library.

Sometimes it works wonders—in the child who is in "over his head."

We'll certainly investigate the possibility. Our son has also experienced trouble reading. One teacher said, "He may be 'dyslexic.'" Do you have suggestions?

Yes. Following the suggestions in this book should help him pay attention and, in so doing, improve his reading skills.

Are there still other things that you recommend?

Yes. One-on-one tutoring using *intensive phonics.*

Intensive phonics?
Tell us more.

By intensive phonics I mean a carefully structured program designed to teach your child the sounds of each letter.* Although such a program may not suit every child, I've seen it help many children.

Are there phonics instruction programs we can use at home?

Yes. There are some very good ones.**

*Obtain *Why Johnny Still Can't Read,* by Rudolph Flesch from your public library.
**See Reading list, Section III for more information.

Nutritional Supplements

Many of the foods and beverages children consume today are loaded with sugar and partially hydrogenated fats and oils. They also contain phosphates, artificial food coloring, additives, insecticides and chemicals of many sorts. These foods are usually deficient in important nutrients and micronutrients, including zinc, calcium, magnesium and the B vitamins.

Cleaning up a child's diet—cutting out the sugar, soft drinks and the packaged and processed foods—will help him obtain many of the nutrients he needs. I also recommend nutritional supplements. Moreover, a number of authorities are now supporting the use of such supplements to fortify the body's immune system and provide "nutritional insurance."

Does Johnny need nutritional supplements?

Yes. Here's why:

Many of the foods and beverages he's been consuming are deficient in important nutrients and micronutrients.

What are some of them?

Vitamins, minerals and the essential fatty acids (EFA's).

What do they do—how do they help?

Like different members of a football team, they play important roles in keeping Johnny healthy.

Give us some examples.

Iron helps children build normal red blood cells and, along with zinc, increases their resistance to infection.

Antioxidants, which include the mineral selenium and vitamins A, C and E, help protect him from environmental pollutants.

Are there still other nutrients that help and what do they do?

Yes. Magnesium, calcium and vitamin B$_6$ help reduce nervous-system irritability. Vitamin C strengthens the immune system. Other B vitamins are also important, as is vitamin D.

We've heard people talk about essential fatty acids. Could you tell us about them?

They're "good" oils. We call them "EFA's," and like vitamins and minerals, they're also members of the nutrient team.

What are some of the symptoms and signs of an EFA deficiency?

Dry, flaky skin or "chicken skin" (bumps on arms, legs and cheeks).

I'm thirsty!

Dry hair.

Excessive thirst.

Hyperactivity.

Allergies.

Johnny has all of these symptoms. What can we do to help him?

Cut down on processed foods, especially those containing white flour and sugar.

Avoid margarine and foods containing partially hydrogenated oils.

Give him salmon or sardines packed in sardine oil at least once a week.

Give him EFA supplements.

What vitamins and minerals do you recommend for your patients?

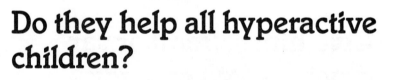

Yeast-free, sugar-free, color-free vitamin-mineral tablets or capsules.

Do they help all hyperactive children?

Most, but not all, hyper-active, inattentive children benefit from these supple-ments.

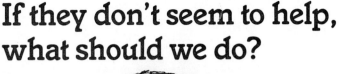
If they don't seem to help, what should we do?

Continue them—unless they disagree.

Any other suggestions?

Some hyperactive children have been helped by larger doses of the B vitamins, especially vitamin B$_6$.

Extra magnesium may also help nervous system irritability.*

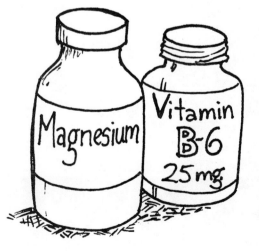

---

*For more information on vitamins and other nutritional supplements, see Section II of this book and pages 180–206 of *Solving the Puzzle of Your Hard-to-Raise Child*.

Section II
More Information

Parents' Experiences

WESLEY'S STORY

"Our son, Wesley, was born May 4, 1979. Between the ages of 2 and 3 months, he was troubled by persistent yeast infections in his mouth and diaper region. At the age of 3 months, he developed his first ear infection—he experienced a dozen such infections in the next 18 months.

"In the spring before he was 18 months old, he began to develop behavior problems. Periodically, he'd go stark raving mad—wild—climbing the walls. Because of these symptoms, we were referred to a psychologist for counseling. Between the ages of 2 and 3, the ear infections and behavior problems continued."

I first saw Wesley in August 1982. He was "all over" the room. He was fiddling with everything on my desk and constantly distracting his mother—and me. I prescribed a comprehensive treatment program which included a yeast-free, sugar-free diet and nystatin.

I saw him again a month later. His mother said, "Wesley is like a different child. However, when I give him sweets or 'junk food' his hyperactivity and irritability return."

At a follow-up visit in May 1983, his mother commented, "Wesley is doing great and we're continuing the diet and nystatin. We only had one outbreak of hyperactivity this past Sunday—at a wedding reception. He ate cake and drank punch. That night he was in terrible shape."

Wesley continued the nystatin in a reduced dose for many months. Yet, he became overactive and irritable if he ate corn or sweets in any quantity.

During a follow-up phone visit with Wesley's mother, Phyllis (2-15-90), she said, "Wesley's doing great. He's in the fifth grade, a B student and reading much better. He's alert, happy and healthy.

"If we turn him loose and he eats more sugar, he develops a bad attitude, becomes fidgety and can't sit still. But when we control his diet, he's a wonderful child."

—Phyllis and Randy

JESSICA'S STORY

"My five-year-old daughter, Jessica, has always been overly active. She could not sit still; she threw tantrums; she would not follow simple directions; she was loud; she was depressed a great deal of the time and a whole lot more.

". . . Jessica had problems with milk from birth. Her projectile vomiting gradually got better as she ate more solid foods. . . . When she was four, I started her in a pre-school kindergarten. After a few months her teacher spoke to me about Jessica's behavior.

"I consulted a behavior specialist but it didn't seem to help. . . . In kindergarten, Jessica was 'up there' most of the time. Also, after being 'up there' she would experience a state of depression.

"A month ago I learned about diet and behavior and put Jessica on an elimination diet. By the fifth day, she was 'a different child' . . . Milk was the first food given back to Jessica. About 30 minutes afterwards, she was 'climbing the walls.' She couldn't sit still and got louder. It took about 2 hours for her to calm down.

"Off milk, *Jessica is like a different child*. She doesn't throw tantrums, jump all the time, talk back or toss and turn all night. Instead she handles situations well, sits quietly, obeys and sleeps comfortably.

"In the last few weeks, I've also held and hugged her more. Before I removed milk from her diet, she could never sit still long enough and she never wanted to be hugged. Now it is her idea. Jessica is beginning to feel good about herself.

"If my husband and I had been made aware of hidden food allergies sooner, Jessica and our whole family could have avoided so many problems.

"But now we're excited over the changes that have taken place and we have hope for a better future for our child and our family."

—Tammy

KRISTIE'S STORY

"When our six-year-old daughter, Kristie, was almost three years old, she began having ear infections—one right after another. During the next year, she developed such severe behavior problems that our pediatrician sent us to a children's hospital and to a child-development center in Louisville. They said Kristie was very bright and when they couldn't find anything wrong, they said, 'She has a behavior problem.' None of their suggestions helped.

"Our pediatrician then sent us to Dr. J. T. Jabbour at LeBonheur Children's Hospital in Memphis. Dr. Jabbour tried different drugs but none of them helped. Then he said, "Her behavior could be caused by something she's eating.""

"In March of 1989, we put Kristie on an elimination diet. On adding foods back, we found that chocolate, sugar, food dyes, yeast and wheat triggered her nervous system symptoms. Then we brought her to you, and because she had so many ear infections, you prescribed nystatin. You also recommended vitamins, magnesium, flaxoil and other supplements. We also took her off packaged foods containing sugar and dyes and fed her well-balanced meals.

"Today our little girl is a changed person. She smiles, giggles and laughs. She's no longer 'klutzy' like she was before. Her sleeping patterns have drastically improved. She's agreeable and her behavior has totally changed. She's doing well in kindergarten and her teachers can't believe she was ever hyperactive.

"The diet and treatment program is so simple I can't believe doctors won't at least try elimination diets first, rather than automatically putting children on drugs. This program has changed Kristie's life and ours, too."

—Cheryl and Stanley

You'll find a brief report of other children like Wesley, Jessica and Kristie under "Management and Discipline" in this section.

Hyperactivity and the Attention Deficit Disorder

"F idgety Phil" and other children who couldn't (or who wouldn't) sit still and pay attention were described in the medical and lay literature over a hundred years ago.* So were children with irritability, incorrigibility, bursts of temper and marked changes in disposition.

Sometimes children who showed such behaviors were labeled as "naughty" or "undisciplined." At other times they were said to be "emotionally disturbed."

In the early 1920s, W. R. Shannon, a Minnesota pediatrician noted that some allergic children were restless, irritable, unruly, peevish, high-strung and difficult to manage. He also noted that these objectionable behaviors subsided and improved following dietary changes. He suggested that these reactions were caused by food sensitivity reactions in the nervous system.**

Since that time, dozens of other physicians have described food-related behavioral problems in children. However, because most of these reports were based on anecdotal observations and were not substantiated by allergy skin tests (or laboratory tests) most physicians have been skeptical of the diet/behavior relationship.

*Medical reprints on hyperactivity, the Attention Deficit Disorder and food allergies are available from the International Health Foundation. To obtain information about these reprints, send a long, SASE (2 stamps) to I.H.F. Box 3494, Jackson, TN 38303.
**Shannon, W. R.: "Neuropathic Manifestations in Infants and Children as a Result of Anaphylactic Reactions to Foods Contained in their Dietary," *American Journal Diseases of Children*, 24:89, 1922.

Personal Observations

In the mid-1950s, six or seven years after I began my pediatric practice, an alert mother convinced me (against my will!) that her child's irritability, fatigue and other symptoms improved when she eliminated milk and chocolate from his diet. About the same time, I read reports in the medical literature by several allergy pioneers,* describing food-induced nervous-system symptoms in children. So I began to look for food sensitivities in my patients and I found a few children with systemic and nervous symptoms who improved when they stopped consuming some of their favorite foods, especially milk.

> **An alert mother convinced me that her child's nervous symptoms were diet-related.**

Soon thereafter, using trial elimination diets (avoiding milk, egg, wheat, corn, chocolate and citrus), I was able to help many more of my patients in my practice who complained of fatigue, headache, short attention span, nasal congestion, abdominal pain, muscle aches and bedwetting. In 1958, I presented my findings on 23 such children at a meeting of the Allergy Section of the American Academy of Pediatrics in Chicago. In 1961, I published my findings on 50 such children in *Pediatrics*** (the official journal of the American Academy of Pediatrics).

Remarkably enough, at the time of this study (the late '50s), my associates and I saw only an occasional child with severe hyperactivity (the child who couldn't sit still, who talked too much and too loud and who was destructive and forever causing problems for his parents, teachers and siblings). However, in the late 1960s and early 1970s

---

*Rowe, A. H.: "Clinical Allergy and the Nervous System," *Journal of Nervous and Mental Disease*, 99:834, 1944. Randolph, T. G.: "Allergy as the Causative Factor of Fatigue, Irritability and Behavior Problems of Children," *Journal of Pediatrics*, 31:560, 1947. Speer, F.: The Allergic Tension-Fatigue Syndrome, *Pediatric Clinics of North America*, 1:1029, 1954. Dees, S. C.: "Neurologic Allergy in Childhood," *Pediatric Clinics of North America*, 1:1017, 1954.

**Crook, W. G. et al,: "Systemic Manifestations Due to Allergy. Report of 50 Patients and a Review of the Literature on the Subject." (Sometimes Referred to as Allergic Toxemia and the Allergic Tension-Fatigue Syndrome.) *Pediatrics*, 27:791-99, 1961.

we began to see more and more inattentive and hyperactive children.

I began to place these overactive children on trial diets and I was pleased to see that most of them improved—often dramatically. I also found that many other dietary ingredients caused problems in these children, especially sugar and the food dyes. Between January 1, 1973, and De-

cember 31, 1977, I saw 182 new patients with the chief complaint of hyperactivity, short attention span and/or related behavior and learning problems.

In 1978 I carried out a questionnaire survey to obtain more information on these children. *One hundred thirty-six (74.7%) parents of the children in this study noted a clear-cut improvement in their child's behavior on an elimination diet. An additional 17 (9.3%) felt their child's hyperactiviy was "probably diet-related."*

The foods causing symptoms in the 136 children with obvious food-behavior reactions included sugar (77), colors, additives and flavors (48), milk (38), corn (30), chocolate (28), egg (20), wheat (15).

*An average of three foods were identified as trouble-makers by parents, and many other foods were listed including peanuts, corn, apple, orange and yeast.**

The Feingold Observations

In 1973, a California allergist, Benjamin Feingold, at a meeting of the American Medical Association, discussed what he felt was an "epidemic" of hyperactive behavior in children. He reported that over half of the hyperactive patients in his practice improved on diets which eliminated

---

*Crook, W. G.: "Can What A Child Eats Make Him Dull, Hyperactive or Stupid?," *Journal of Learning Disabilities*, 13:53-58, 1980.

artificial colors, flavors and preservatives and the salicy-late containing foods.*

However, in spite of the effectiveness of the Feingold diet, skeptics said, in effect, "Children improved because of the extra attention they're receiving. Diet plays little or no role in contributing to hyperactivity." Moreover, they cited "scientific studies" to support their point of view.

Why were these studies negative? Most of them investigated only the role of food colors and they failed to look at other dietary ingredients, including milk, sugar and other foods. In commenting on these studies, Dr. Doris Rapp said, "If a child limps because five nails in his shoe are sticking in his foot and only one nail is removed, he'll continue to limp."

Information From Lay Organizations

From Canada: In 1980, the Allergy Information Association, 65 Tromley Dr., Suite 10, Etobicoke, Ontario, M9B 5Y7, conducted a reader survey. Fifty of the fifty-two parents who responded were absolutely certain that diet

---

*Salicylate-containing foods include almonds, apples, apricots, all berries, cherries, cloves, coffee, cucumbers and pickles, currants, grapes and raisins, green peppers, nectarines, peaches, plums, prunes, tangerines, tomatoes and all teas. Further information can be obtained from the Feingold Association of the United States (FAUS), Box 10085, Alexandria, Virginia 22310.

played an important role in contributing to their child's behavior and learning problems. Food dyes, milk and other dairy products led the list of offenders. However, other dietary ingredients were also incriminated.

Following dietary elimination, only six of the fifty-two children continued to require medication to control their hyperactivity and/or attention deficits.

From Australia: In December 1989 I received a detailed report from Olive Tompson, Administrator, Hyperactive Help, #4 Crocker Way, Innaloo, Western Australia 6018. This report contained a survey of hundreds of parents of hyperactive children conducted from June 1987 until October 1988. Food colors, additives, preservatives, dairy products, sugar and many other foods caused problems. So did environmental chemicals.

In discussing her experiences during the past ten years, Mrs. Tompson said, *"Many parents of hyperactive children are unable to find anyone, professional or otherwise to help them. And disturbed children of today may be well on their way toward being tomorrow's criminals. If children cannot be helped and controlled before they get to school age, what hope do we have of correcting the damage in later years?"*

From England: In February 1990, Sally Bunday, secretary, The Hyperactive Children's Support Group, sent me a detailed report. Here's a summary of what she had to say:

"The dietary ingredients which cause hyperactivity obviously vary from child to child. The main problem items we find include:

"Food coloring and other additives, dairy foods, salicylate-containing foods, wheat, sugar and yeast. We also find that *Candida albicans* causes problems for the majority of children, especially those who have had antibiotics, or whose mothers have had antibiotics and yeast infections. We also feel that toxic chemicals and nutritional deficiencies cause problems.

"It's important for parents to know that although the worst symptoms in hyperactive children fade as the children get older, without some intervention when they're young, they'll continue to have problems. These include: depression, school failure, lack of confidence, social problems and trouble with the law."

Support for the Relationship of Diet to Hyperactivity

For over two decades, C. Keith Conners, Ph.D., Professor of Medical Psychology, Duke University Medical Center, has carried out research studies on children with hyperactivity and attention deficits. In a recent articles, "How Food Affects Behavior and Learning"*, Conners commented,

"... Careful reading of the scientific literature reveals that the links between food and behavior are complex, and not as easily dismissed as many people would like to think. There are, in fact, several significant ways that foods become involved in behavior and learning in children, some less obvious than others."

In his articles Conners also discusses that controversial subject of sugar and its role in causing hyperactive behavior. He said,

"My findings . . . encourage us to regard the problem of sugar as still open and needing more investigation."

Conners also referred to the work of Dr. Bonnie Kaplan in Canada and to the "oligoantigenic diet" which he said "has recently shown to be beneficial for a wide variety of children's behavioral and physical complaints."

In a report in a leading British medical journal,

---

*From CHADDER, Spring/Summer, 1990, published by CH.A.D.D., Suite 185, 1859 N. Pine Island Rd., Plantation, Florida 33322. (305) 587-3700. Dr. Conners has also written a book, *Feeding the Brain: How Foods Affect Children*, New York: Plenum Press, 1989.

J. Egger, M.D. and associates (Department of Immunology and Child Psychiatry, Institute of Child Health and Hospital for Sick Children, London), told of their findings in studying 76 selected overactive children.* *All children were put on an elimination (few foods) diet. Sixty-two of the children improved and a normal range of behavior was achieved in 21 of these youngsters. Other symptoms including headache, abdominal pain and fits, also often improved.* Dr. Egger published further reports on his findings in the *Journal of Pediatrics* in January 1989.**

Also during 1989 a Canadian team of researchers reported that half of a group of 24 preschool-age, hyperactive boys improved on elimination diets with negligible placebo effects.***

Medication for Hyperactivity

In the mid-1930s, Charles Bradley, M.D., found that Benzedrine, a stimulant medication, had the opposite affect on the behavior of a number of hyperactive children. It helped them settle down and pay attention. During the next several decades, a related medication, Dexedrine, was also found to be effective.

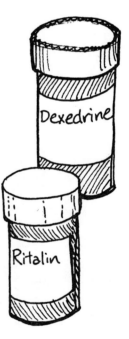

During the mid-1950s, another stimulant medication, methylphenidate (Ritalin), appeared on the scene, and because it helped control symptoms and caused fewer side effects, its use has increased rapidly during the last 20 years.**** Today many physicians feel it should be given to all (or at least most) hyperactive, inattentive children. Although Ritalin is effective in controlling symptoms, many parents are concerned.

Here's why:

---

*Egger, J., Carter, C. M., Graham, R. J., Grimley, D. and Soothill, J. F.: *The Lancet*, March 9, 1985, 1(8428) 540-45)

**Egger, J., Carter, C. M., Soothill, J. F. and Wilson, J.: *Journal of Pediatrics*, 114: 51-58, 1989.

***Kaplan, B., McNicol, J., Conte, R. Moghadam, H. B.: *Pediatrics* 83:7, January 1989.

****A report in the October 21, 1988, issue of the *Journal of the American Medical Association*, Daniel J. Safer, M.D. and John M. Krueger, M.D., M.P.H., said, "Since 1971, the Baltimore County Health Department has conducted surveys which show that the percent of public *elementary* school students receiving medication for hyperactivity and inattentiveness, rose from 1.07% to 5.96%. The rate of medication treatment has grown steadily since 1971, doubling on the average of every 6 to 7 years. *Medication treatment for hyperactive children in the United States has emerged from its minor treatment role in the 1960's to become a dominant child mental health intervention in the late 1980's.*"

They feel that medications are being used indiscriminately as a sort of "quick fix" for the child with complex behavior and learning problems. Evidence of their concern is expressed in articles the *Wall Street Journal*, the *Los Angeles Times, USA Today, Newsweek, MacLeans Magazine* and other publications.

Pediatric leaders have also expressed concern over what they feel to be the overuse of Ritalin. Here's an excerpt of a statement by the Committee on Children with Disabilities, Committee on Drugs of the American Acad-

emy of Pediatrics.* "Stimulant therapy is considered by some to be a panacea or cure-all. . . . *Medication for children with ADD should never be used as an isolated treatment.* Proper classroom placement, physical education programs, behavior modification, counseling and provision of structure should be used before a trial of pharmaceutical therapy is attempted."

Yet, the committee FAILED to say, "Diet plays an important role in causing hyperactivity and before Ritalin is prescribed for any child, dietary factors should be carefully evaluated."

In his book *The Difficult Child*, Stanley Turecki, M.D.,** said,

> "Critics rightly charge that Ritalin is over-prescribed . . . often not monitored carefully . . . On the other hand, claims that it is a dangerous chemical straitjacket, a sinister plot to impose behavioral control so as to make life easier for lazy teachers and uncaring parents, are certainly excessive and sensationalistic.

"Claims that it is a dangerous chemical straitjacket . . . are excessive and sensationalistic." —Stanley Turecki, M.D.

> "Proponents correctly point out that Ritalin clearly improves attention span and disruptive behavior . . . and that it is relatively safe. However, there exists too often an attitude of the 'quick fix,' a tendency to view medication as a specific 'cure' for an established 'condition' . . .
>
> ". . . If the child's family and school are in a state of crisis, the temporary use of Ritalin can reverse the situation and create an atmosphere of greater calm, which in turn will allow the parents and the teacher to institute a program of improved management. Once things are going better, the medication can often be discontinued."

In discussing allergy and special diets, Turecki said, "There is a core group of children whose behavior improves with dietary regulation, and elimination of the

---

*"Medication for Children with an Attention Deficit Disorder." A report of the Committee on Children with Disabilities, Committee on Drugs, American Academy of Pediatrics, 1986-87, *Pediatrics:* 758-760, November 1987.
**Turecki, S. with Tonner, L.: *The Difficult Child* (revised edition), Bantam Books, New York, NY 1989, pages 230-232.

offending agents helps children with established allergies. . . . In general, proper nutrition obviously is desirable. More particularly, a sound diet appears to be the key to a healthy immune system . . . Even if the pediatrician points out there's insufficient scientific evidence, I've heard enough stories of improvement to feel that parents shouldn't be discouraged from pursuing a dietary approach. . . . A reputable nutritional specialist is the person to consult."

The Prognosis of Children Who Receive Only Ritalin

Esther H. Wender, M.D., speaking at an American Academy of Pediatrics (AAP) Medical/Science Writers Conference (July 19, 1989), stressed that medication alone will not likely improve hyperactive children's long-term outcome, without other forms of treatment—such as remedial education approaches, psychotherapy and altered behavior on the part of the caregivers.

> According to an AAP press release Dr. Wender said, "These drugs, the only form of biological treatment consistently effective in the majority of children with Attention Deficit Hyperactivity Disorder (ADHD), produce only a temporary change in behavior while the medication is in the child's system. This recurrence of symptoms when the medication wears off or is discontinued can usually be expected, but is frequently misunderstood.
> "Dr. Wender said that although side affects are seen commonly, the common ones are not serious and the serious ones are reversible when the medication is discontinued. Often the consequences of medication are confused with the consequences of the disorder. . . .
> "While symptoms improve with medication, the child still behaves somewhat differently than normal children the same age. . . . Some children outgrow the syndrome, but most continue to have symptoms into adolescence or early adulthood. Many end up with antisocial disorders or chronic underachievment."

In a 1987 article, James H. Satterfield* and associates described the results of two prospective longitudinal studies of predelinquent, Caucasian hyperactive boys treated with Ritalin and/or other stimulant medications.

---

*Satterfield, J. H., Satterfield, B. T. and Schell, A. M.: "Therapeutic Interventions to Prevent Delinquency in Hyperactive Boys," *Journal Am. Acad. Child. Adol. Psychiat.*, 1987, 26, 1, 56-64.

Eighty of these boys received drug treatment only (DTO). Fifty other boys were put on a program of "multimodality treatment" (MMT) for 2 to 3 years. This program was a combination of Ritalin and "intensive" cognitive-behavorial-interpretive treatments based on an individual treatment plan for each child.

Boys in the MMT group were much less apt to be arrested for felony crimes (15% as compared to 43% in the DTO group). In addition, none of the boys in the MMT groups were institutionalized (compared to 22% of the boys who received DTO).

Therapeutic Interventions to Prevent Delinquency in Hyperactive Boys

JAMES H. SATTERFIELD, M.D., BREENA T. SATTERFIELD, M.S., L.C.S.W., AND ANNE M. SCHELL, PH.D.

Abstract. Results of two prospective longitudinal studies of predelinquent hyperactive boys are presented. The ... was a study of 80 Caucasian hyperactive boys treated with stimulant medication and the second a study of ... hyperactive boys treated with multimodality treatment (MMT). The two groups were well matched ... variables. Official teenage arrest and institutional rates were found to be significantly lower ... group. These findings demonstrate the importance of long-term evaluations in ... ...dicapping childhood disorders and suggest that MMT in childhood is a cost-... ...ncy prevention in hyperactive boys. *J. Amer. Acad. Child Adol. Psychiat.,* ... ...OH, delinquency treatment, prevention.

"*... the hyperactive group had more conduct problems and drank more alcohol than non-hyperactive adolescents who had school difficulties ... Generally, clinical treatment with Ritalin was found to have no beneficial effect and there was some evidence to suggest a poor behavior outcome for the drug treated group.*" (Blouin)

"*... although methylphenidate (Ritalin) continued to improve the child's behavior at home and at school, it did not significantly alter poor long-term academic performance, delinquent behavior, or poor emotional adjustment.*" (Weiss, 1975)

"*... effective delinquency prevention programs for all hyperactive boys would be less expensive than the cost of institutionalization for those who, without such treatment, would become institutionalized.*"

most drug studies have been continued for a few weeks or, at most, months.

A few studies have examined outco... (2-5 years) in drug-treated b... Rappaport (1976) ... boys who...

...onger periods ... Riddle and hyperactive antidepres-... ...ously with dropouts ...peractive ... contin-... ...ractive ...t seem ...nd to ...ance ...rom ...ro-... to ...t

Men... examine the... with hyperactive c... delinquency. The two typ... compared are stimulant drug trea... (essentially a drug-treated-only (DTO) group) and a combined treatment approach that included stimulant drugs and intensive psychological treatments (multimodality treatment (MMT) group).

As noted by Rutter (1981) the criteria for successful treatment of children with chronic handicapping disorders, such as the hyperkinetic syndrome, must include the fostering of normal development as well as the removal of symptoms of abnormal behavior. Most therapeutic studies of hyperactive children have not included the fostering of normal development as a criterion for successful treatment. The most widely studied and currently used treatment for hyperactive children is stimulant medication. Although drug studies have demonstrated that stimulant medications are undoubtedly effective in reducing many symptoms of hyperactive children, they have not demonstrated long-term benefits, such as enhanced normal development (Barkley, 1977). This is largely because

...eutic interventions ...opment of teenage ...d intervention to be ... plus brief counseling

...n ...si... that phet... come childn... second ...ved chlorpromaz...ine for 18 months to 3 years. The authors concluded tha'... tinued to improve the chi'... it did not significantly a... ance. delinquent beh...

Blouin and co... study, compar... school diffic... adolescen... lems ar... lesce... ph... reg... "Gene... no benefi... poor behavio... et al., 1978). We have previou... for a group of 110 DT... subjects to be discussed h... term outcome for this DTO s... by others of a substantial subg... adolescent youths (Huessy et al.,

...methyl-... ...ore favorable out-... ...atched groups of hyperactive ...oup received no medication and the ...ough methylphenidate con-... ...r at home and at school, ...m academic perform-... ...nal adjustment. ...year follow-up ...ren who had ...d that at ...prob-... ...do-...

Received Nov. 21, 1983; revised April 2, 1985 and Aug. 14, 1985; accepted Aug. 15, 1985.
Dr. Satterfield is Executive Director of the National Center for Hyperactive Children, where Breena T. Satterfield is Clinical Director. Anne M. Schell is with the Department of Psychology, Occidental College, Los Angeles, CA 90041.
Supported in part by NIMH Grant MH-37344.
Reprints may be requested from Dr. Satterfield, National Center for Hyperactive Children, 5535 Balboa Blvd., #215, Encino, CA 91316.
0890-8567/87/2601-0056 $02.00/0 © 1987 by the American Academy of Child and Adolescent Psychiatry.

56

Reproduced by permission, John F. McDermott, Jr., M.D., Editor

However, no difference was noted in the incidence of "minor offenses" in the boys in the two groups. These offenses included petty theft, alcohol intoxication, vandalism and possession of less than one ounce of marijuana.

Satterfield also stated,

"We found juvenile delinquency rates, as reflected by official arrests and institutionalization rates, to be 10 to 20 times greater in our hyperactive DTO group than in the normal control group (i.e., non-hyperactive boys). Duration of drug treatment was not related to delinquency outcome. . . . Thus, it seems clear that long-term outcome findings for DTO children are fairly discouraging."

In discussing his studies, Satterfield said their assessments suggest that "a fairly lengthy period of childhood treatment is crucial to an optimal outcome." He also stated that, "our findings have certain cost-effectiveness implications with respect to delinquency-prevention programs for hyperactive children. . . . MMT may result in 33 fewer institutionalizations per 100 hyperactive youths treated. Cost of institutionalization* is approximately $30,000 a year vs. a $3,000 annual cost for MMT."

*Institutional care in a psychiatric hospital is even more expensive and ranges from $18,000 to $24,000 each month.

In my opinion, any safe therapy that can keep a teenager out of an institution is obviously worthwhile. So I commend Dr. Satterfield and his associates for their carefully documented observations showing that long-term, intensive counseling programs help predelinquent young men and also save money.

Yet—at the same time I must say, "Please take a fresh look at the relationship of diet to nervous system symptoms in hyperactive, inattentive children *before* beginning a long-term trial of medication and psychiatric care."

In their article, Satterfield and associates also reviewed the studies of others. Here are excerpts:

> "The most widely studied and currently used treatment of hyperactive children is stimulant medication. Although drug studies have demonstrated that stimulant medications are undoubtedly effective in reducing many symptoms of hyperactive children, they have not demonstrated long-term benefits such as enhanced normal development." (Barkley, 1977)

Another study compared hyperactive children with children who had school difficulties, but no hyperactivity. These investigators found that at adolescence, the hyperactive group had more conduct problems and drank more alcohol than the non-hyperactive adolescents who had school difficulties. In comparing a group of hyperactive children who were treated with Ritalin and a group who did not receive this medication they stated, *"Generally clinical treatment with Ritalin was found to have no beneficial effect and there was some evidence to suggest a poor behavior outcome for the drug treated group."*[*]

A two-year study of 72 drug-treated hyperactive children in 1976 by Riddle and Rapoport[**] ". . . provided evidence that medicated hyperactive boys continue to be at high risk for academic and social difficulties and that medication's long-term effect is mainly suppression of impulsive and hyperactive behaviors."

In still another study of 26 hyperactive children treated with Ritalin, Weiss[***] and co-workers, found that

---

[*]Blouin, A. G., et al: "Teenage Alcohol Use Among Hyperactive Children. A 5-year Follow-Up Study," *Journal Pediatric Psychology* 3:188-194, 1975.

[**]Riddle, K. D. and Rapoport: "A 2-year Follow up of 72 Hyperactive Boys," *Journal Nerv. Ment. Dis.*, 162:126-134, 1976.

[***]Weiss, G.: "Long term outcome of the hyperkinetic syndrome" *Developmental Neuropsychiatry*, ed., M. Rutter, New York: Guilford Press, Chap. 20.

while this medication "...continued to improve the child's behavior at home and at school, it did not significantly alter poor long-term academic performance, delinquent behavior, or poor emotional adjustment."

It is clear from these observations that the long-term prognosis of children with hyperactivity and attention deficits is dismal—even frightening. Ritalin does help control the symptoms in hyperactive, inattentive children.* Psychological counseling also helps. Yet, none of the studies cited above investigated the role of diet.

My thoughts on the use of Ritalin: *Over 75% of the hundreds of hyperactive children I've treated during the past 20 years have NOT required Ritalin to control their hy-*

Over 75% of my hyperactive patients did not require Ritalin.

---

peractive and/or inattentive behavior. Yet, I have prescribed it occasionally, in "crisis" situations (such as those described by Dr. Turecki). Here's an example:

> Johnny, 6½ years old, came in with his distraught mother, Sarah, who said, "I simply can't cope with this child's behavior any longer. Neither can his father. Johnny's teachers are threatening to kick him out of school. They've had it too."

> Johnny was "all over" my office. He was the most "hyper" youngster I'd seen in a long time. His mother also appeared anxious, and tearful. Devastated. When my nurse associate, Nell Sellers, and I began talking about a carefully planned diet, Sarah said, "I'm not up to it at this time."

Because I felt that Sarah wouldn't be able to do an elimination diet correctly, or get the support and cooperation from family members, I prescribed Ritalin. Along with this medication, Nell and I gave Sarah lots of warm reassurance. We said,

> "Although we don't have a "quick fix" we think we can help you. Here are materials for you and your husband to

---

*The experience of professionals is mixed on the use and need for medication. Some have found that their hyperactive patients (especially those with allergies) will improve—often dramatically—on a comprehensive treatment program which does not include medication. By contrast, they have observed that non-allergic children with the Attention Deficit Disorder, without hyperactivity, may require Ritalin (or other medication) for optimum results.

read. Here's a prescription for Ritalin that will help Johnny settle down so they won't throw him out of school."

Happily, within 48 hours after starting the Ritalin, Johnny was better. Much better. And as Johnny's behavior improved, Sarah's anxiety lessened. Moreover, Johnny's performance at school improved, thereby lessening the frustrations of his teachers.

In the weeks and months that followed, Johnny's family was able to carry out an elimination diet and identify a number of food troublemakers including artificial colors, sugar and milk.

Artificial colors, sugar and milk contributed to Johnny's hyperactivity.

Because Johnny gave a history of repeated ear and sinus infections and had taken many antibiotics, he was also placed on nystatin. In addition, he was given lots of "psychological vitamins." After several weeks Ritalin was discontinued with no flare up in symptoms.

In this patient, Ritalin was used as a temporary "crutch" which enabled the family to settle down and deal with the causes of their child's problem.

Concluding comments: Ritalin helps relieve symptoms in hyperactive children. Long-term counseling and psychiatric care also lessen the severity of the disorder. *Yet, based on my observations, and the observations of others cited in this book, nutritional, allergic, toxic (and other) causes of hyperactivity should be investigated before a child is placed on Ritalin or referred for psychiatric care.*

Cleaning Up the Diet

Like most folks, you're likely to eat many of your meals "on the run." And for many families, this includes McDonalds, Wendy's and other fast-food "eateries".

You're also bombarded by TV, radio, newspaper and magazine ads encouraging you to eat or drink a particular product. And even though these ads now contain phrases like "natural," "lite," "high fiber," and "low cholesterol," you're confused. Such confusion is understandable.

It doesn't make things easy when you go to the supermarket with your children after a hard day's work. And while you're looking for vegetables, fruits and other wholesome foods, they're apt to wander over to the cereal section and bring back a box of Froot Loops or Trix, and say, "Mama, please buy this."

Being a parent, making a living and feeding yourself and your children do present challenges for you and other families in the '90s. But changes already underway can make things easier for you. These include a growing interest in better nutrition and a greater concern about the environment. Also included is an increasing availability of "organically grown" foods which are relatively free of chemicals.

How can you improve the quality of your child's diet? Become a nutrition "authority."* Who is an "authority"? *An authority is a person who knows more about a subject than most other people.*

How do you become an authority? You read and study.

Suggestions to Help You Get Started

1. Write to the Center for Science in the Public Interest (CSPI), 1875 Connecticut Ave., Suite 300, Washington, D.C. 20009. I've been a CSPI member for the past 14 years, and in my opinion it is the best source of nutrition information available in America today. Their publications include:

   a. The *Nutrition Action Healthletter* (published 10 times a year). It is informative, profusely illustrated and easy to read. Titles in recent issues include "A Discussion of Alar and Other Chemicals in the Food," "How's Your Diet—Take the CSPI Nutrition Quiz," a delightful feature on the back cover of each issue is a review of "Thumbs Up Foods" (the good ones) which are called "The Right Stuff" and "Thumbs Down Foods" which are called "Food Porn."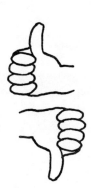

   CSPI and its affiliated organization, Americans for Safe Food (ASF), are also working to make the American food supply free of pesticides. Here are

*You'll find additional information in Section III.

excerpts from an article by Ann Montgomery, "America's Pesticide Permeated Food", which was published in the June 1987 *Nutrition Action Healthletter.*

"Industry and government propaganda holds that America has the 'safest food supply in the world' . . . but a lot of what's sold isn't safe at all . . . unfortunately, the very foods that health conscious consumers are trying to eat more of—fresh fruits and vegetables—are those that are most likely to be contaminated. . . .

You won't see dangerous residues on any ingredient list . . . the law doesn't require it.

"It's time to turn back the clock and take a close look at safer, non-chemical methods of growing, storing and preserving crops—before the environment and our food supply become even more contaminated with persistent toxic residues."*

Other publications available from CSPI-ASF include a 50-page booklet, *Guess What's Coming to Dinner*, published by ASF in 1987. Here are excerpts:

"Our food is contaminated. From pesticide residues on fruits, vegetables and grains to antibiotic resistant strains of Salmonella bacteria in our meat, to traces of powerful animal drugs in poultry, invisible chemicals and germs permeate our food supply. . . . You won't see these dangerous residues on any ingredient list. . . . the law doesn't require it . . .

". . . Consumers feel betrayed. Having learned about the dietary cause of heart disease, cancer and diabetes, millions of Americans have been eating more fish and poultry, whole grains, fresh produce and low-fat dairy products. All too often, however, these otherwise wholesome foods are tainted and government regulations amount to little more than a false promise of protection. . . .

". . . Once consumers learn about the dangers associated with so many of our foods, the next step is to press for safe alternatives. A growing demand for safe food will eventually causes grocers and farmers to make changes. . . . Here are a few of the suggestions in this booklet under the heading, "What Can You Do?":

1. Organize an Americans for Safe Food coalition in your community (write to ASF to find out how).

*For a copy of this article send a SASE adn $2.00 to CSPI at their Washington address.

2. Get informed, then organize a local "Safe Food Day" community forum or public debate on contaminants in food.

3. Prepare a list of local sources of contaminant-free food.

4. Write, and tell your friends to write, letters to the editor of your local newspaper. The shorter your letters, the more likely they are to be published.

The Daily Gazette
Anytown, State
USA

2. Write to Mothers and Others for Pesticide Limits, 40 W. 20th St., New York, NY 10011. This organization is a project of the National Resources Defense Council, co-chaired by Meryl Streep and Wendy Rockefeller. It is working to call attention to the problem of pesticides in food, to press for a reform in pesticide regulations and enforcement, and to assure safe produce is widely available around the country. In 1989, this organization published an attractive, beautifully organized, informative, 86-page book, *For Our Kid's Sake—How to Protect Your Child Against Pesticides in Food*. Here are a few excerpts from this book:

"The amount of pesticides used in the U.S. has multiplied ten-fold since the 1940s and has doubled in the past two decades alone. More than 2½ billion pounds of pesticides are now used each year—on agricultural crops, in forests, on ponds and lakes and city parks, in lawns and in homes . . .

"At least 17% of the country's 18 million 1 to 5 year olds are being exposed to neurotoxic organophosphate pesticides.

Millions of children are being exposed to neurotoxic pesticides.

These pesticides are designed to poison an insect's nervous system and can cause nervous system damage or impair the behavioral system in humans . . . They're found in foods in levels above what the Federal government considers safe.

"The problem of pesticides in food is particularly serious in children for several reasons. For one thing, children consume proportionately more fruits and vegetables—and therefore more pesticides—than adults."

I have no data to show that pesticides (or other chemicals) play a significant role in the "epidemic" of children with ADD and hyperactivity, but certainly such a relationship is possible. Even if your child isn't hyperactive or inattentive, feeding him safer foods and joining "Mothers and Others" is a great idea.

3. Join Natural Food Associates (NFA). This nonprofit, educational organization was organized over 30 years ago to work for the production and use of organically grown foods. Such foods are free of pesticides and other toxic chemicals. The address is P.O. Box 210, Atlanta, TX 75551. A $15 membership fee will include a one-year subscription to *Natural Food and Farming*, the official journal of this organization.

The food a child eats influences his behavior.   **Louise Bates Ames, Ph.D.**
The Gesell Institute

---

4. Read the superb 1988 book, *Super Immunity for Kids*, by Leo Galland, M.D., with Dian Dincin-Buchman, Ph.D. In the Foreword, Louise Bates Ames, Ph.D., commented, "The food a child eats influences his behavior. . . . This book is exciting. . . . It could change the eating habits of a whole generation of children."

5. Read my comments on pages 29-80 of *The Yeast Connection Cookbook—A Guide to Good Nutrition and Better Health*. In this book I compare a person's body to an automobile and point out that if a car doesn't have proper fuel it won't run. And your child's body won't "run" properly if it doesn't receive proper fuel. I especially emphasize the importance of more complex carbohydrates, including vegetables, fruits and whole grains. I also suggest diversifying your child's diet with the grain "alternatives," amaranth, quinoa and buckwheat.

6. Read *The Brown Bag Cookbook* by Sarah Sloan. Mrs. Sloan served as the Food Service Director, Fulton County (Atlanta, Georgia) public schools for 31 years. In talking to parents, she said in effect, "Let your children help you in the kitchen . . . teach them to cook. Children will eat anything and everything they fix for themselves."

7. Read Chapter 30, "What is a Good Diet?" in my book, *Solving the Puzzle of Your Hard-to-Raise Child*. In this chapter I discuss amino acids, essential fatty acids, minerals, vitamins, fiber, fresh vegetables, grains, fruits, nuts, seeds, eggs, dairy products, unrefined vegetable oils and lean meat.

Special Recommendations for Professionals and Parents Concerned About Nutrition and the Environment

Read the magnificent new 735-page book by Joseph D. Beasley, M.D. and Jerry Swift, M.A., *The Kellogg Report—The Impact of Nutrition, Environment and Lifestyle on the Health of All Americans*. Although I haven't read every page of this book, I highly recommend it for anyone concerned about the life and health of all Americans—including our children. (Available from the Institute of Health Policy and Practice, Bard College Center, 221 Bardway Plaza, Suite 301, Amityville, NY 11701. $30 postpaid.) A condensed version of this book is being published by Random House in mid-1991.

Read the 1988 book, *Choose to Live*, by Joseph D. Weissman, M.D. (Grove Press, 920 Broadway, New York, NY 10010). This book is beautifully researched by a physician with impeccable scientific credentials. Although it's written mainly for adults, if you follow the suggestions it contains, you'll live a longer, healthier and happier life and be better able to care for your child.

Dr. Weissman points out that fruits, vegetables and grains are contaminated by insecticides and chemicals* of various sorts. Yet, he's even more concerned about animal foods including meat, milk and eggs. Here's why:

All animals are "bioconcentrators and biomagnifiers." Here's what happens. Toxic materials which are deposited in farming areas are eaten by the animals and then concentrated stored in their muscle and fat tissues. (See illustration.)

Sources of Pesticide Residues in the U.S. Diet

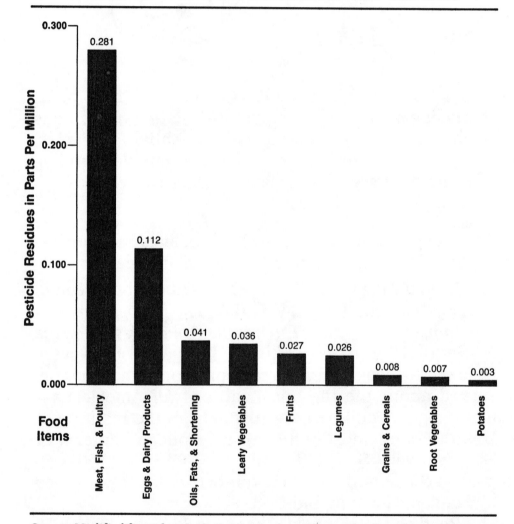

Source: Modified from data in G. Q. Lipscomb and R. E. Duggan, "Dietary Intake of Pesticide Chemicals in the U.S.," *Pesticides Monitoring Journal* 2 (1969): 162-69; and P. E. Cornelliussen, "Pesticide Residues in Total Diet Samples," *Pesticides Monitoring Journal* 2: (1969) 140-52: (1872) 313-30.

---

*Lead and other toxic substances can cause learning problems in children. In an interview with Deborah Norville on the Today Show (November 6, 1990), investigators from Virginia reported that lead is found in the drinking water of many schools. (see also pages 199-203), Solving the Puzzle of Your Hard-to-Raise Child)

Cleaning Up Your Child's Environment

Unless like Rip Van Winkle, you've been peacefully sleeping for the past 20 years, you know that we're poisoning our planet. Here are a few examples:

Millions of barrels of poisonous chemicals are buried in dump sites all over the country. These toxic substances leach into our ground-water supplies. Weed killers, insecticides and other chemicals are sprayed on farms. Other chemicals are sprayed on fruits and vegetables to improve appearance or delay ripening. Insecticides and other chemicals are found in greater concentration in meat, poultry, eggs and dairy products because after consuming insecticide-laden foliage and other food, animals concentrate the toxic substances and store them in their fat tissues.

We're also polluting our oceans to such an extent that we can no longer eat fish and seafood without saying to ourselves, "I wonder if this fish contains mercury or other toxins?"

Air Pollution in Your Home

The pioneer Chicago allergist and environmental medicine specialist Theron Randolph warned, "While outdoor air pollution is a significant source of exposure—indoor air pollution poses an even greater threat." Similar warnings were made by Nicholas Ashford, Ph.D., Claudia Miller, M.D., Lance A. Wallace, Ph.D., and other speakers at the January 1990 Annual International Symposium in Dallas, Texas, on "Man and His Environment in Health and Disease."

In his presentation, (and in a report published in the *Journal of the American Medical Association*), Dr. Wallace, a scientist at the U.S. Environmental Protection Agency, stated that "A decade of research on human exposure to toxic and carcinogenic organic chemicals has shown that exposure is usually due (to) . . . consumer products and building materials. These findings have upset the ideas that most exposures are due to such outdoor sources as chemical plants, incinerators, hazardous waste sites and automobiles."

Household pollutants listed by Wallace included cigarette smoke, cosmetics, pesticides, dry-cleaned clothes and laundry and bathroom chemicals.

Indoor air pollution* is especially dangerous for you and your children because exposure is so constant. Here are a few suggestions for reducing it:

---

*A superb new book on this subject, *Clean and Green—The Complete Guide to Non-toxic and Enviromentally Safe Housekeeping,* by Annie Berthol-Bond. Available from Ceres Press, P.O. Box 87, Woodstock, New York 12498. $10.95 postpaid.

1. Don't smoke and don't let people smoke in your home. Children in homes where people smoke experience twice as many respiratory infections as children in smoke-free homes. Respiratory infections are treated with antibiotics; these drugs knock out friendly bacteria while killing enemies; candida yeasts proliferate in the gut and contribute to other health problems. (See Ear Infections, Antibiotics, and The Yeast Connection.)

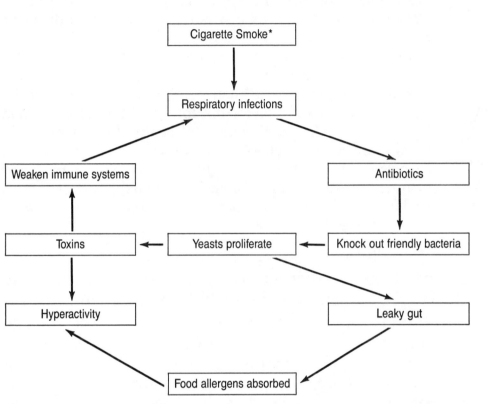

2. Don't spray insecticides in your home. Volatile sprays that poison bugs can adversely affect your children. Use instead roach powders which contain 99% boric acid, produced by several different manufacturers and obtainable from most supermarkets or health food stores. Use only as directed.

3. Don't use odorous toxic or potentially toxic substances in your home. Substances which may cause problems and provoke symptoms in your child include floor cleaners, waxes, laundry chemicals, bathroom chemicals, air fresheners and most colognes and perfumes. Especially those which are made from synthetic sources.

---

*and other chemical pollutants

Air Pollution in Your Child's School

In an article from the January 21, 1988, *Toronto Star*, entitled, " 'Chemical Soup' in the Classroom," staff reporter Tracey Tyler said, "Air pollution is causing health problems ranging from headaches to rashes to brief loss of memory." Here are excerpts from Tyler's article:

> "Don and Debbie Morton vow to keep their son, Ryan, 7, out of his Etobicoke Public School until air pollution is cleaned up. The boy became 'hyper' and his marks dropped as his school's carbon dioxide count rose and mould levels jumped to twelve times the limit considered tolerable . . .
>
> " 'A child doesn't really have a recourse,' says environmental consultant Bruce Small. . . . Small conducted a major study of school pollution for the Toronto Board of Education 3 years ago. He found 97 sources of health threatening pollutants in 27 Toronto schools. These included carbon dioxide, carpet glue, fumes from art supplies, felt pens, cockroach and termite sprays, brush cleaner, floor polish, particle board shelving, neighborhood industrial pollution, photocopy paper and the fumes from school buses."

Your child's resistance resembles a rain barrel. And chemicals in his environment are like pipes draining into the barrel. When he is exposed to many chemicals, his barrel overflows and he develops symptoms. Yet, you can do something and every little bit helps. After you've cleaned up the chemical exposures in your home, visit your child's school.

What you can do: Don't let the size and scope of environmental problems discourage you. You can do something, and every little bit helps. Visit your child's school. Talk to other parents. Join your local PTA. Inquire about bathroom ventilation and the use of odorous chemicals in the school.

Sources of Information About Chemical Pollutants in Our Air, Soil and Water

Environmental Action, 1525 New Hampshire Ave., N.W., Washington, DC 20036. This national political lobbying and education organization publishes a bimonthly magazine. Membership is $20 a year (includes cost of the magazine).

Human Ecology Action League, Inc., P.O. Box 49126, Atlanta, GA 30359-1126. This volunteer organization publishes a quarterly magazine, *The Human Ecologist*. Local chapters in various parts of the country provide information for people with chemical sensitivities.

The Delicate Balance, the publication of the Environmental Health Association of New Jersey, 1100 Rural Avenue, Voorhees, NJ 08043.

Citizens Clearing House for Hazardous Waste, Inc., P. O. Box 926, Arlington, VA 22216.

Environmental Health Association of Dallas, P. O. Box 226811, Dallas, TX 75222. This organization publishes a bimonthly newsletter. Supscription rate is $20.

The National Foundation for the Chemically Hypersensitive, P. O. Box 9, Wrightsville Beach, NC 28480.

Foundation for Advancement in Science and Education (FASE), 4801 Wilshire Blvd., Suite 215, Los Angeles, CA 90010.

Adapted from William Rea M.D. Used with permission.

Television

Research studies have shown that the average American child spends more hours in front of the TV set than he spends at school. Here's more about the adverse effects of television on hyperactive children:*

1. It encourages children to eat junk food. Judith J. Wurtman, Ph.D., a mother and a biologist at the Massachusetts Institute of Technology, declared:

    > "Television advertising is probably the most persistent force undermining good eating habits. Messages that promote well balanced meals and nutritious foods tend to be overwhelmed by the huge number of ads that appear during prime TV time for children."**

2. It contributes to violent and aggressive behavior.***

3. It causes physiologic changes and ridicules traditional family values. According to an article in the December 1989 issue of *Focus on the Family*****, in responding to a reader who expressed concern about the violent con-

---

*See also pages 32-34, 269-272, 303-304 of *Solving the Puzzle of Your Hard-to-Raise Child*.
**Wurtman, J., quoted in *Jane Brody's Nutrition Book* (New York: W.W. Norton, 1981), page 386.
***Gore, T.; *Raising PG Kids in an X-Rated Society*, (Nashville: Abingdon, 1987).
*****Focus on the Family*, Pomona, CA 91799.

tent of some children's television cartoon shows, Dr. James Dobson stated,

> "Studies have measured actual physiological changes that occur when a child is watching a violent television program or movie; the pulse quickens, the eyes dilate, the hands sweat, the mouth goes dry and breathing accelerates."

Although Dr. Dobson didn't say that television encourages hyperactive, aggressive, or violent behavior, I've seen reports which suggest such a relationship.

In his continuing comments, Dr. Dobson said,

> "Try to steer your children toward alternative forms of entertainment. I know it's a scarce commodity, but there is still some good television to be found—if you look for it. Public stations and certain carefully selected cable services are a good place to begin your search.

A VCR allows you to select video entertainment that comes into your home.
James Dobson, Ph.D.

> "Besides educational television programs they often carry re-runs of some of the older TV series that date from a time when the family and traditional values were held in higher regard. A VCR has advantages too—it allows you to select and control the kind of video entertainment that comes into your home. There are already a number of fine Christian videos for children available on the market."

In a previous issue of *Focus on the Family* (November 1989), Duncan and Priscilla Jaenicke stated that the most alarming aspect of TV's assault on American families lies in its ability to mold our children's values. And they quoted Christian educator V. Gilbert Beers who warned,

> "Our children are being turned over to electronic parents (who give our kids) a new and different heritage by ridiculing our values.
>
> "No parent would open his doors to a bunch of strangers and say, 'Here are our kids, come on in, say anything you want!' Yet, we are advocating, to total strangers, the responsibility to teach our kids."

4. It causes many other adverse health affects:
   a. Children who stay indoors and look at TV are deprived of the beneficial effects of natural sunlight

and skylight. Research studies carried out in Sarasota, Florida, schoolrooms showed that children in classrooms illuminated by fluorescent lights were more hyperactive than children in rooms with "full-spectrum" lights.* Of course, outdoor light provides the best full-spectrum light.

b. It interferes with outdoor exercise. According to reports in the *San Diego Tribune* (January 13, 1982) exercise, including running, jumping and field exercises helped lessen hyperactivity in many children. And some hyperactive youngsters who participated in vigorous programs of exercise were able to stop medication.

c. Children are exposed to more electromagnetic radiation, especially if they sit closer than 8 feet from the set.

d. Children looking at TV snack more and tend to consume nutritionally deficient foods and beverages.

Suggestions for Controlling TV

1. Make it clear to your children where television fits into the list of family priorities.

2. Make sure the child understands that other things are more important than television:
   a. homework
   b. exercise
   c. sleep
   d. daily chores
   e. family time

3. Don't put your TV set near the dining room table where it curtails conversation.

4. No "flipping" of the channels just to see what's on.

*Ott, J.N.; *Light, Radiation and You,* (Old Greenwich, CT: Devon-Adair, 1982.), pp. 130-133.

Other comments: In an article, "Choose, Watch TV Programs Together," in the April 7, 1990 issue of the *Knoxville News-Sentinel,* staff writer Ina Hughes said:

"Despite conflicting studies and statistics, professional and lay groups concerned about children and the media agree on one thing: Guidelines at home are at least as important as guidelines in the television industry.

"Parents become part of the problem or part of the solution, depending on how involved they are and the quality and quantity of what comes into their home over television.

"Dr. Robert Mendelson, chair of the Committee on Communications of the American Academy of Pediatrics, says the ideal solution is for parents and children to set aside time each week to decide together what programs they will watch.

" 'Sunday night is a good night to do this', says Mendelson. 'Get out the TV schedule for the week and pick two hours a day . . . to watch. The average child watches between 22 to 28 hours of TV a week. Two hours a day cuts that almost in half.' "

Recommendations by Mendelson: (1) Television should not be turned on until all homework and chores have been done. (2) Parents should watch television with their children. Mendelson says, "You can even learn from bad television. Parents can talk about what is happening on a certain show or ask what this commercial or that commercial is getting at. A lot can be learned from these kinds of conversations between parents and their children." (3) The most damage is done when parents use television as a babysitter. "There is just nothing that positive about TV. There's no way to justify passively watching whatever happens to catch their fancy at the moment."

I agree with all of Dr. Mendelson's recommendations. I especially like his suggestion for making out a schedule once a week for watching TV. In this way, you can plan TV viewing just as you would for a holiday meal at Grandmother's, a ballgame or a trip to a zoo.

Allergies

Allergy has been recognized for thousands of years. But it wasn't until 1906 that the Austrian pediatrician, Von Pirquet coined the word "allergy." He put together two Greek words—*allos*, meaning "other" and *ergon*, meaning "action." To Von Pirquet, the term allergy meant "altered reactivity."

Most people feel that allergy means "hypersensitivity to a substance which in a similar quantity doesn't bother other people." Incidentally, that's the definition you'll find in the Webster's New World Dictionary. However, if your child is bothered by allergies, and you move from one city to another, you may run into different ideas about allergy—how it is defined, how it is diagnosed, and how it should be treated.

> *Immunological mechanisms are important but they don't tell the whole story.*
> **Frederic Speer, M.D.**

Many allergists say, "The term *'allergy'* should be limited to those conditions in which an immunological mechanism can be demonstrated." But others feel that the allergic diseases are much broader in scope. The late Dr. Frederic Speer of the University of Kansas said, "While immunological mechanisms are undoubtedly important in explaining allergic diseases, they don't tell the whole story."

Types of Allergies

When your child develops an allergy to something he breathes, such as grass pollen, animal danders or house dust mites, the cause of his symptoms can be suspected

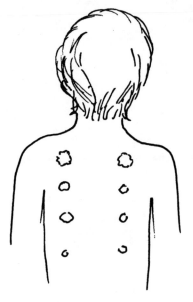

from his history and identified through the use of the simple allergy skin test.* In carrying out such a test, the physician scratches or pricks your child's skin and applies a small amount of an allergy extract.

If your child is allergic to the test substance in the extract, as for example, bermuda grass or cat dander within a few minutes, an itching bump or welt that looks like a mosquito bite will pop up on his skin. Skin testing will cause similar welts if your child is allergic to foods such as egg, peanuts or strawberries. However, if your child is obviously sensitive to these foods, skin tests aren't needed to identify them. Moreover, skin testing of foods that have caused severe reactions can be dangerous.

> ## Your child is apt to be sensitive to some of his favorite foods.

There are other types of food allergies and sensitivities you need to know about. Such allergies have been called "hidden," "masked," "variable," or "delayed onset" food allergies. Allergies of this type are caused by foods your child eats every day. You'll probably be surprised to learn that your child is apt to be sensitive to some of his favorite foods. Moreover, he may be "addicted" to foods which are making him hyperactive and/or inattentive. Like the cigarette or narcotic addict, he's apt to settle down after he's eaten some of the foods to which he's allergic.

Controversy over Allergy

Many subjects you've heard about all of your life are considered "controversial." Included are religion, politics, education, abortion and many others. What's more, if you read *USA Today* you'll see opposing opinions on different issues expressed on the editorial page every day. Food allergy is another such controversial topic.

I became interested in food allergy over 30 years ago when the mother of 12-year-old Mac, convinced me (against my will) that removing cow's milk from Mac's diet helped him feel better, act better and perform better in school.

---

*In vitro (blood) tests are also used by many allergists to help them evaluate inhalant sensitivities in their patients.

About the same time I read two articles in the *Pediatric Clinics of North America** which described nervous system symptoms in children. One of the articles from the University of Kansas described children with the *Allergic Tension-Fatigue Syndrome*. Children with this disorder were at times irritable, nervous and inattentive. Yet, at other times they were tired, drowsy and depressed. Nearly all these youngsters showed dark circles under their eyes, a stuffy nose and other symptoms, including headache, abdominal pain and muscle aches. In each child described by the author, the elimination of one or more common foods resulted in significant and even dramatic relief of symptoms.

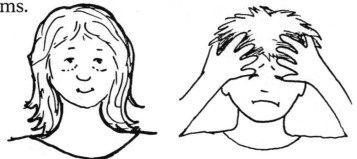

The second article by Dr. Susan Dees* of Duke University described a wide variety of nervous system symptoms in children (and adults) which were food related. And she reported one patient who had shown abnormal "brain waves" (electroencephalographic changes) and convulsions while drinking milk. When the child was taken off milk, the brain wave test returned to normal and there were no further seizures.

During the next several years, I saw dozens of children with the allergic tension-fatigue syndrome in my regular practice. I reported my findings on 50 of these tired, irritable, inattentive youngsters in the official journal of The American Academy of Pediatrics in 1961. Milk and chocolate were major offenders, yet sensitivity to other foods also caused symptoms, including nasal congestion, headache, abdominal pain, muscle aches and bedwetting.

Since that time, I've helped thousands of my patients with systemic and nervous system symptoms, (including hyperactivity and the attention deficit disorder) using

---

*Dees, S. C.: "Neurologic Allergy in Childhood", *Pediatric Clinics of North America*, 1:1017, 1954. and Speer, F.: "The Allergic Tension-Fatigue Syndrome," *Pediatric Clinics of North America*, 1:1029, 1954.

elimination diets. Yet, most physicians have expressed skepticism and one prominent allergist said:

> "Rational physicians cannot accept the tension/fatigue syndrome and the other systemic manifestations which are claimed to be due to food allergy, until we prove on scientific immunologic grounds that food is responsible for these reactions."

And another observer stated,

> "Behavioral disturbances as a manifestation of food allergy have never been demonstrated conclusively."

Increasing Medical Support

In spite of this controversy, in the past two decades a number of academic physicians have described the relationship of diet to many common health problems seen in children. Here are comments from pediatricians who have described the relationship of diet to a variety of systemic and nervous system reactions in children:

John W. Gerrard,* professor of pediatrics (emeritus), University of Saskatchewan, described the reactions of Tim, who had been placed on a restricted diet for 2 weeks and then given a glass of milk to drink and in an hour a second glass. According to Dr. Gerrard—

> "Tim promptly became a ball of fire. He went wild and was quite uncontrollable. . . . At first I found it hard to believe that harmless foods could so change a child's personality; but many parents have made confirmatory, unsolicited observations, and I'm now fully convinced that in ways we do not yet understand, the allergic child's, and adult's too, behavior can be altered and modified as dramatically by foods as it can be altered by drugs."

---

*Gerrard, J. W.: *Understanding Allergies* (Springfeld, IL: Charles C. Thomas, 1973), pp. 14-17.

> ### *The allergic child's behavior can be altered as dramatically by foods as it can be by drugs.* John Gerrard, M.D.

Twenty years ago, several physicians at the University of California, San Francisco, in discussing the tension-fatigue syndrome (TFS), said,

> "Any one of the components of the TFS may be the patient's chief complaint. We've seen patients with this syndrome who were investigated for a brain tumor because of headaches, or studied for anemia because of pallor and fatigue. . . . *Two patients were referred to a psychiatrist because of their behavior.*"*

Frank A. Oski,** professor and chairman of the Department of Pediatrics, Johns Hopkins School of Medicine, in his book, co-authored by John D. Bell commented:

> "Most people, including physicians, believe that allergies to foods produce only such classical symptoms as skin rashes, respiratory symptoms, or gastrointestinal disorders. There's a growing body of evidence, however, to suggest that certain allergies may manifest themselves primarily as changes in personality, emotions, or in one's general sense of well being . . ."

> ### *. . . certain allergies may manifest themselves primarily as changes in personality . . . .* Frank Oski, M.D.

In his continuing discussion, Dr. Oski describes children with the tension-fatigue syndrome and he said,

> *"These children will appear restless and in a constant state of activity. They fidget, grimace, twist, turn and just never seem to sit still. Many of these children are also excessively irritable and can never be pleased."*

Walter Tunnessen, Jr., an associate of Dr. Oski, in discussing the manifestations of food allergies, stated:

> "The culprits I find most often are milk, chocolate and eggs, although cane sugar, corn and wheat should also be con-

---

*Bullock, J. D.: Deamer, W.C., Frick, O. L., Crisp, J.R.,III, Galant, S. P., Ziering, W. H.: "Recurrent Abdominal Pain" (Letters), *Pediatrics*, 46:969, 1970.
**Oski, F. and Bell, J. D.: *Don't Drink Your Milk*, Mollica Press, Ltd., 1914 Teall Ave., Syracuse, NY 13203. 1977 and 1983. pp. 85-88.

sidered. Removing these foods from the diet a few at a time, for a week or two, is all that is necessary. Should the child improve, the eliminated foods are reintroduced. If the symptoms recur over a few days to a week, the foods are again eliminated. Relief of symptoms further supports the diagnosis.

. . . "The manifestations of food allergy are legion. Motor symptoms may include overactivity, restlessness, clumsiness; sensory tension may be reflected in irritability, insomnia, or hypersensitivity to pain or noise. Fatigue symptoms include tiredness, achiness and the like. . . . Pallor, infraorbital circles and nasal stuffiness are almost invariably present. Headache, abdominal pain, enuresis, increased sweating and salivation and infraorbital edema (puffiness and circles under the eyes) are commonly present.

"Obviously, all symptoms and signs are not present in each patient and as mentioned above their subjective nature makes the technologically oriented members of our profession gasp in disbelief. I, too, had been a Doubting Thomas until my son responded to dietary elimination.*"

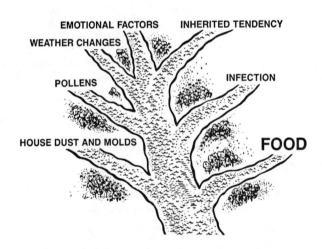

Allergies and Hypersensitivities

Food Allergies and Elimination Diets Come into the Mainstream

In the subtitle of her article in the *New York Times*, (April 29, 1990), "Food Allergies: A Growing Controversy," health columnist Jane Brody said,

"Millions of Americans say certain foods make them sick. Are doctors paying close enough attention?"

---

*Tunnessen, W. W., Jr.: "An 8-year Old Boy With Lethargy and Fatigue," *Clini-Pearls*, Vol. 2 No. 6, July/Aug. 1979, page 3.

Brody briefly summarized the reactions of seven individuals who experienced food-related symptoms. One of these she said was . . .

"yours truly (who) suffered periodic attacks of abdominal pain and swelling that would last for days until dietary sleuthing revealed foods made with soybeans or dried peas as the likely cause."

In her continuing discussion, Brody said,

"The 7 of us are among the estimated 30 million Americans who experience adverse reactions to foods, reactions that most non-medical people call food allergies."

An estimated 30 million Americans experience adverse reactions to foods.
Jane Brody

When she discussed the controversy among physicians, she said,

"In researching this article I initially believed that most of the claims attacking this food or that as the cause of everything from hair loss to athlete's foot were elaborate hokum. But after looking at the medical research and learning about various people's experiences, I now wonder whether the rigid thinking of some doctors is not ill advised. Indeed, in dismissing symptoms that don't involve the immune system, these doctors might be doing a disservice to the health and well being of millions of Americans.

Certainly foods might . . . send some children into an orbit of hyperactivity.
Jane Brody

"Perhaps a food doesn't have to affect the immune system in order to ignite a yeast-infection, cause the sinuses to fill, aggravate arthritis or bring on irritable bowel syndrome. Certainly foods might make some people feel tired or mentally foggy or send some children into an orbit of hyperactivity." *

---

*Reprinted in the July/August 1990 edition of the *Saturday Evening Post*.

Early in 1987 a comprehensive new book appeared on the medical scene, *Food Allergy and Intolerance.** This book, was favorably reviewed in the *Journal of the American Medical Association*, and contains contributions from 83 physicians and other scientists. Here are comments from the Preface:

> "Food allergy is an exciting, challenging, exasperating and sometimes controversial subject. Its study should be a clinical science with diagnosis based on a combination of clinical observations and scientific investigations ....
>
> There has been a strong tendency for the conventional physician to say that if the mechanism is not understood, then food allergy does not exist. ... This is of course unacceptable. ... *The cornerstone of diagnosis of food intolerance is the removal of that food from the patient's diet with concomitant improvement (or not) of the patient's symptoms and their reappearance on adding that food back.*"

The elimination/challenge diet is the Gold Standard for diagnosis.

In another recent report from the Cleveland Clinic, headache, the tension-fatigue syndrome and hyperkinesis were listed as manifestations of food allergy.** Pediatrician Sami L. Bahna, M.D., chairman of the Foundation's Department of Allergy and Immunology said, "Food allergy seems much more prevalent among children than adults."

In a continuing discussion of this subject, the article stated,

> "The majority of food sensitive patients cannot be diagnosed through—routine tests. Dr. Bahna considers the elimination/challenge test the 'Gold Standard' for diagnosis. Once the offending food or additive is identified, management is usually straightforward and successful. Treatment consists primarily of dietary avoidance."

---

*Brostoff, J. and Challacombe, S. J.: *Food Allergy and Intolerance*, Balliere Tindal, E. Sussex England, W. B. Saunders, Philadelphia, 1987.
**Food and Additives Sensitivity Present Diagnostic Dilemma. *Consult—A Forum for Physicians*, The Cleveland Clinic Foundation, Vol. 7, No. 3, April, 1988, pages 8-9.

New Tests for Food Allergies

These include the ALCAT test, which I first learned about from Douglas H. Sandberg, M.D., professor of pediatrics at the University of Miami, and from Jonathan Brostoff of England (co-author of the 1987 book, *Food Allergy and Intolerance*). Here's a brief description of the ALCAT test:

> Blood is drawn by your physician or a laboratory and sent to ALCAT Diagnostic Systems, 19100 W. Dixie Hwy., Miami, FL 33180. The blood is then incubated with dozens of common foods. This test electronically measures the size and number of blood cells both before and after blood is exposed to food extracts. According to Dr. Sandberg, alterations in these blood cells correlate well with clinical disease associated with eating a particular food. Your physician can obtain further information by calling 1-800-225-2658.

Still another test, the ELISA/ACT test, may help identify allergic and adverse food reactions of several types. Your physician can obtain more information by writing to the Serammune Physicians Lab Service, 11100 Sunrise Valley Dr., AMSA Bldg., 2nd Floor, Reston, VA 22091. (703)-255-1157 or 1-800-553-5472.

New Therapies for Food Allergies

These include an oral medication, cromolyn (Gastrocrom, Fisons), which prevents the absorption of allergy-causing foods from the digestive tract. Also, food vaccines or extracts are being used in treating patients with food sensitivities. Although this type of treatment is considered "controversial" and unproven by the American Academy of Allergy and Immunology, Joseph B. Miller, M.D.***, 5901 Airport Blvd., Mobile, AL, 36608; and Doris Rapp, M.D.**, 1421 Colvin Blvd., Buffalo, NY 14223 and other physicians have found these extracts effective in treating thousands of their patients.

---

*Miller, J. B.: *Relief at Last*, Charles C. Thomas, Springfield, 1987.
**Rapp, D.: *The Impossible Child*, Practical Allergy Research Foundation, Buffalo, New York, 1986.

The Relationship of Allergy to Hyperactivity and Learning Disabilities

Hyperactivity, learning disabilities and allergies are commonly seen in the same child. Yet, I've known hyperactive youngsters who made A's in all their subjects—except behavior and deportment.

I've seen other hyperactive youngsters who had none of the usual symptoms of allergies (nasal congestion, skin rashes, cough, fatigue or dark circles under their eyes).

Similarly, I've seen thousands of allergic children who are calm, well-behaved youngsters. Moreover, most of these youngsters performed well in school—on a par with their peers.

Nevertheless, *most of my hyperactive patients have been troubled by allergies and learning disabilities.* Such disabilities have often developed in children with normal intelligence because their allergies and hyperactivity interfered with their performance.

THE RELATIONSHIP OF HYPERACTIVITY AND LEARNING DISABILITY TO ALLERGY

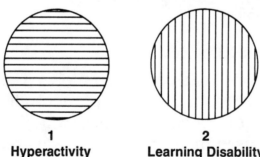

1
Hyperactivity

2
Learning Disability

3
Allergy

1. A hyperactive child with no allergy or learning disorder.
2. A learning disabled child (with no hyperactivity or allergy).
3. An allergic child (with no learning disability or hyperactivity).
4. A hyperactive learning disabled child.
5. An allergic learning disabled child (without hyperactivity).
6. An allergic hyperactive child (without learning disability).
7. An allergic hyperactive child with a learning disorder.

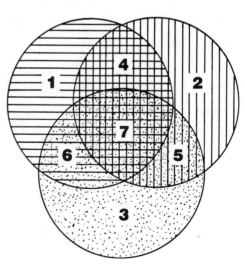

Parables About Allergy

Confucius say, "A journey of a thousand miles starts with one step." Overcoming your allergies, like the journey Confucius was talkng about, requires many steps. Maybe not a thousand, but many.

Dr. Susan Dees of Duke University, in talking about allergies some years ago, said in effect,

> "The more the allergic person knows about himself and the things he's sensitive to, and the more he knows about allergies and how they affect him, the better are his chances of overcoming them."

To help you understand more about allergies, especially food allergies, study the parables on the next few pages. Each one illustrates one or more important principles about allergy.

The first parable, *Timmy and the Allergy See-Saw* will help you understand the concept of *allergic load*. Your child's allergic symptoms may be caused by many different substances ("gremlins"), including foods, pollens, house dust, mites, molds and animal danders.

In addition, he may be sensitive to tobacco smoke or chemical fumes which increase his allergic load. Emotional stress, chilling, viral, bacterial or yeast infections can also increase his chances of developing symptoms.

If you understand the story of Timmy, and can identify his allergy "gremlins" and how he keeps them under control, you'll have a better chance of overcoming your allergies.

The second parable, *Susie's Cow's Milk Allergy*, illustrates several important principles which will help you understand and manage hidden or delayed-onset food allergies. Here they are:

A. Hidden food allergies are caused by foods your child eats every day. When he eliminates them, his symptoms will usually clear up within a week.

B. If he eats the food again, following this short period of elimination, his symptoms will usually return promptly.

C. If he avoids a food troublemaker for 4 to 8 weeks (or longer), he'll usually regain some tolerance to the food.

S	M	T	W	T	F	S
1	2	3	4	5	6	7
8	9	10	11	12	13	14
15	16	17	18	19	20	21
22	23	24	25	26	27	28
29	30	31				

↖ MILK DAY

D. After his sensitivity to the food lessens, he can usually eat the food occasionally (such as every 4 to 7 days) without causing symptoms.

E. Yet, if he eats the food every day—especially in large amounts—his tolerance will break down and the symptoms will return.

THE STORY OF TIMMY AND THE ALLERGY SEE-SAW

Timmy, like most other allergic youngsters, is sensitive to things he eats, breathes or touches.
Ear infections, yeast overgrowth and chemical fumes may also add to his allergic load.

We'll call these trouble-makers "gremlins."

pollens

tobacco smoke

foods

molds

animal danders

chemical fumes

dust mites

emotional stress

chilling

infection
(viral, bacterial and yeast)

In spite of his allergies, Timmy sits still in school and is happy and free of symptoms most of the time.

Here's why: His parents control the "gremlins" so that his allergy resistance is usually greater than his load of "gremlins."

Allergy Resistance

Allergy Load

Here are examples:

Although Timmy is allergic to milk, he can drink an occasional glass or eat ice cream at a party without getting sick.

Allergy Resistance

MILK

↑ Allergy Load

Allergy Load →

RAGWEED

Timmy can go through the ragweed season with few symptoms if he doesn't drink milk or play in a field full of ragweed.

↑ Allergy Resistance

But if Timmy drinks milk during ragweed season, his allergic load overcomes his tolerance or resistance.

As a result, he's apt to develop allergy symptoms, including: wheezing, fatigue, irritability, sneezing, hyperactivity or headache.

Timmy's allergy tolerance can also be overcome if he drinks a lot of milk any time during the year, or—

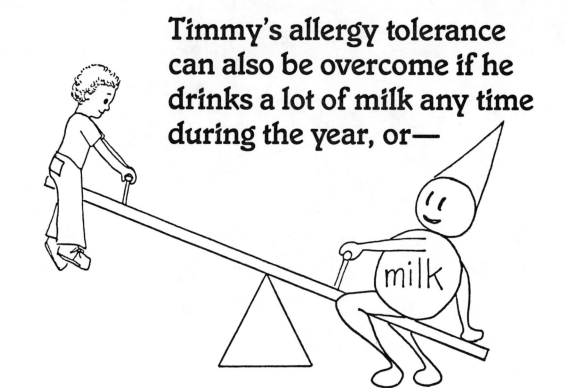

if dust collects in his room, his pet sleeps on the foot of his bed and he's drinking milk.

It can also be overcome in many other ways.

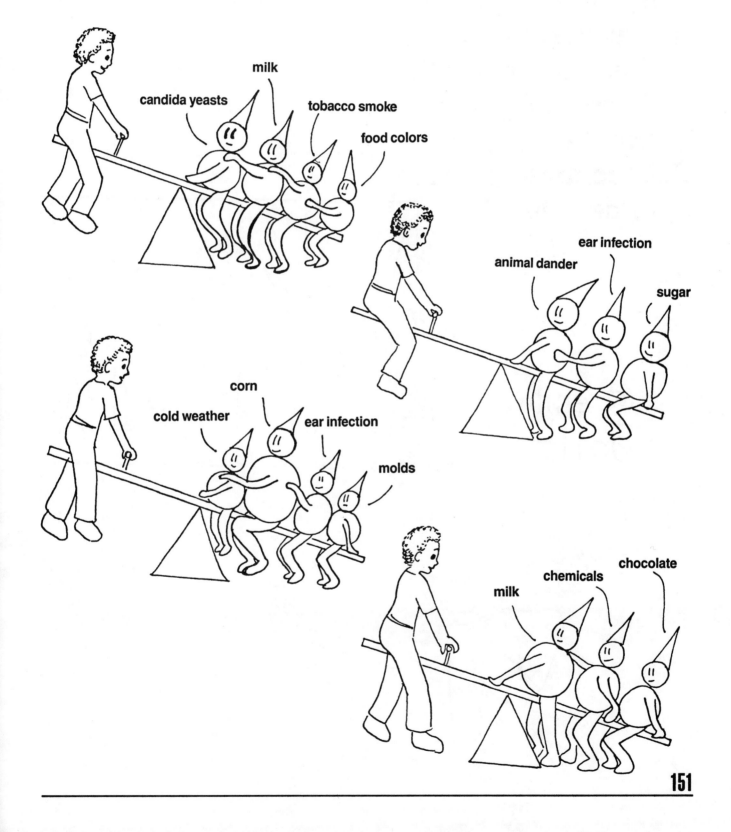

The best way to keep
Timmy, and your allergic
child, well, calm, happy
and attentive is to . . .
1. Find out which allergy
   "gremlins" give him
   trouble.
2. Keep these "gremlins"
   under control.

Gremlin
Jail →

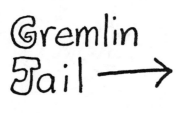

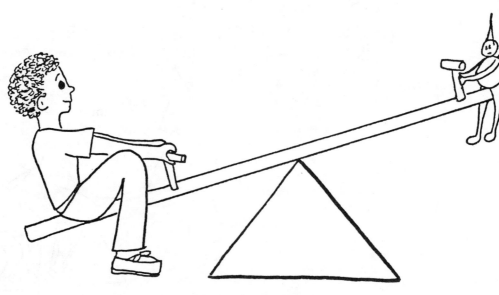

SUSIE'S COW'S MILK ALLERGY

When Susie was an infant her mother nursed her and gave her only breast milk for many months.

Susie thrived. She was happy and healthy. No colds, no skin rashes. And Susie rarely cried.

When Susie was nine months old, her mother weaned her and gave her cow's milk from a cup.

After a few weeks Susie developed a cough, cold and ear infection.

Although Susie's doctor prescribed several kinds of medicine, her symptoms persisted.

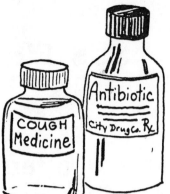

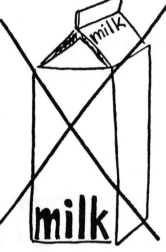

Then one day the doctor said, "Susie may be allergic to cow's milk. Don't give her milk for the next week and see what happens."

After three days Susie was better. And in six days her symptoms vanished.

Several days later Susie's mother gave her milk. By bedtime her nose was running and she coughed all night.

The milk was stopped. In two days Susie's "cold" dried up and she felt fine.

Susie drank no milk for six months. Then one day, her mother gave her milk and nothing happened.

Mon.	Tue.	Wed.	Thu.	Fri.
1	2	3	4	5

But when Susie drank milk five days in a row,

her cough, cold and irritability returned.

Susie again avoided milk (this time for a year). And now she can drink milk once a week and it doesn't bother her.

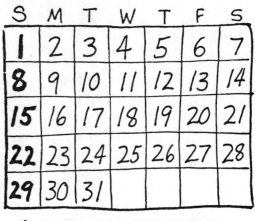

↰—MILK DAY

Allergy to milk (or to *any* food) is like a fire

that dies down

Yet blowing on the embers (like eating a lot of the food) will cause the allergy to return.*

*Adapted from William C. Deamer, M.D., University of California, San Francisco

Elimination Diets

T hanks for these meal suggestions go to Jean Smith, R.N. Foods listed on these menus contain no milk, egg, wheat, corn, sugar, citrus, yeast, food coloring or additives.

MENUS

Breakfast Suggestions*

Toasted rice crackers with "all-fruit" spread and/or roasted almond butter, sliced bananas or other fruit.

Grilled pork chop, sautéed** apple or pear slices with a dash of cinnamon.

Bowl of brown rice with added nuts or fruit. You may also add sugar-free fruit spread.

Bowl of oatmeal topped with fresh fruits. (Strawberries, raspberries, peaches, etc.) Add fruit spreads or pecans (or other nuts).

Pineapple and strawberries, sliced turkey, cold or grilled.

*Hearty eaters may need to combine different breakfast suggestions.
**Sauté in olive, canola, sunflower, safflower or flaxseed oil.

Special pancakes or waffles topped with all-fruit syrup or applesauce.

Sliced cantaloupe, ground-beef patty, sliced potatoes. Special diet breads.

Muffins, flatbreads and pancakes made from potato mix, rice mix, brown rice mix, barley mix*, nut butters and/or fruit spread.

Lunch Suggestions, Including School Lunches

Homemade soups:
Beef vegetable
Chicken and rice
Chicken and quinoa
Chicken and kale with or without onions

Salads:
Tuna, grape, nut salad
Tuna, apple, nut salad
Chicken/turkey salad with grapes, apples, nuts or celery

Fresh fruits:
Apples
Bananas
Pears
Grapes
Berries
Peaches
Watermelon
Pineapple
Cherries

*These mixes can be ordered from Allergy Resources, 195 Huntingdon Beach Dr., Colorado Springs, CO 80921. (1-800-873-3529)

Vegetables:
Vegetable sticks with or without dips
Celery
Carrots
Zucchini
Cucumber

Sandwiches (using acceptable homemade
    bread):
Turkey
Chicken
Beef
Pork
Tuna
Game
Dress with tomato, lettuce and acceptable
    mustard

Other foods:
Trail mixes
Home roasted nuts
Pumpkin seeds
Acceptable pancakes rolled with almond or
    cashew butter with fruit spread or banana
May be used on rice crackers

Acceptable potato chips or taro chips*

---

*Do not contain additives, preservatives, colorings, saturated fats or other chemicals.

Main Meals

Sliced pork roast or grilled pork chops
Baked sweet potato
Black-eyed peas
Sliced bananas with strawberries

Baked, grilled or roasted chicken
Rice
Lettuce, tomato, cucumber salad
Peach slices
Kiwi

Baked or grilled fish*
Steamed broccoli or cabbage
Grated carrot and pineapple salad
Acceptable bread**

Wild game, i.e., venison, duck
Brown rice
Green peas or greens
Fresh fruit cup (berries, grapes, plums)

Grilled or roasted turkey
Fresh spinach and tomato salad or wilted
    spinach***
Sliced potatoes or quinoa
Slices of watermelon or honeydew melon

Grilled shrimp, crab or beef patty
Baked potato
Green beans or asparagus

Baked or grilled rabbit, chicken
Squash and onions
Steamed broccoli or brussels sprouts

---

*Can use batter made of oat or amaranth flour
**Made from oat flour, barley flour, rice or buckwheat without eggs, milk or yeast. (See recipes)
***Heated in skillet in tablespoon of oil until wilted.

Snacks

Unprocessed nuts*
Green pepper slices
Carrot sticks
Celery sticks
Zucchini sticks
Acceptable potato or potato chips

Fresh Fruits except citrus:
Pineapple spears or chunks
Strawberries
Cherries
Nectarines
Grapes
Apples
Pears
Berries
Peaches

Other foods:
Apple or banana slices with roasted almonds
    or roasted cashew butter

Acceptable muffins with nut butters or fruit
    spreads

Dips, nut butter dip, tomato salsa dip

Puffed rice and nut butter balls

Homemade trail mixes

---

*Unprocessed nuts can be slow roasted in a 250 degree oven in toast pan—stir every 10 to
15 minutes until roasted. May be lightly salted.

FURTHER DIET DETECTIVE WORK MAY BE NEEDED

If you identify several foods which trigger your child's hyperactivity—and he continues to experience symptoms caused by something he's eating or drinking—you'll have to search further.* Here are suggestions:

Try the "Caveman Diet" for a week. *On this diet, your child avoids every food he eats more than once a week.* When he shows convincing improvement, lasting 48 hours, return the eliminated foods to the diet, one food per meal. Foods he can eat on this diet include:

Meats: lamb, turkey, fish, lobster, and wild game

Fruits: Cantaloupe, mango, kiwi, pineapple, watermelon, strawberries, blackberries, blueberries

Vegetables: Sweet potato, broccoli, carrots, asparagus, cauliflower, celery, cabbage, cucumber, radish, greens

---

*If your hyperactive child continues to experience puzzling food-related reactions, salicylate-containing foods (including apples, apricots, berries, grapes, raisins and tomatoes) may be the culprits. You can obtain more information about salicylate-free diets from the Feingold Association of the United States (FAUS), Box 10085, Alexandria, VA 22310.

Beverages: Bottled mineral water or spring water

Nuts (unprocessed): Any but peanuts

Oils: Olive oil, mineral oil, sunflower or safflower oil

Grain alternatives: Buckwheat, amaranth, quinoa, teff

YOU'LL NEED TO KEEP A DIARY

To tell if your child's elimination diet makes a difference, you'll need to keep a diary.

Buy an 8x10 inch notebook and use a new page each day. Begin the diary three days before you start eliminating foods, and continue it until the diet is completed.

Grade your child's symptoms:
0—no symptoms
1—mild symptoms
2—moderate symptoms
3—severe symptoms

Here are examples: If he sniffs or his nose runs all the time, put "2" in the respiratory column for each period during the 24 hours.

If he is calm when he wakes up and becomes irritable and overactive after eating breakfast, put a "0" in the "before breakfast" and a "3" in the "after breakfast" column.

If he complains of a bad headache on arising each day, which gradually disappears by lunchtime, put a "3" in the headache column "before breakfast," a "2" in the morning column and put a "0" in the headache column for the rest of the day.

At the bottom of the page, list the foods eaten each day.

By keeping this diary, you can usually tell which foods . . . if any . . . are causing his complaints.

SYMPTOM AND DIET DIARY

SYMPTOMS	TIME OF DAY				
	Before Breakfast	After Breakfast	After Lunch	After Supper	During Night
Hyperactive or irritable					
Tired or drowsy					
Headache					
Respiratory (stuffy nose, cough, etc.)					
Digestive (belly ache, nausea, etc.)					
Muscle and joint symptoms					
Other					

	Breakfast	Morning	Lunch	Afternoon	Supper	Evening
WHAT YOUR CHILD ATE TODAY						

HELPING YOUR CHILD STAY ON THE DIET

Carefully plan your child's elimination diet. Ask other family members to help. Purchase and prepare the foods. These steps are essential. Equally important is obtaining your child's cooperation. Here's how Mary's mother did it.

As she thought about the diet, she said to herself, "Mary likes orange juice, frosted junkies and chocolate milk for breakfast; hot dogs and corn chips for lunch; and a cola after school. . . . She isn't going to like this diet . . . And I may run into trouble getting her to cooperate and not cheat."

Then Mary's mother had an idea—a bright idea. She said to her husband, "Mary loves games and prizes (and what child doesn't?), so I'll make a game out of the diet."

Here's what Mary's mother did. She made a chart and taped it to the door of the refrigerator. Then she bought a box of stars for Mary to paste on the chart.

She told Mary about the diet, saying, "Mama is going to buy extra special foods for you to eat for the next two weeks. And we're going to play 'the diet game'."

Mary's Diet Game Chart

	Monday	Tuesday	Wednesday	Thursday	Friday	Saturday	Sunday
Breakfast	☆	☆					
Morning	☆	☆					
Lunch	☆	☆					
Afternoon	☆	☆					
Supper	☆	☆					
Evening	☆	☆					

"What kind of game is that?" asked Mary. "And how can I win prizes?"

Mama replied, "By eating foods . . . like a hamburger patty and sliced potatoes for breakfast; bananas, peanut butter and rice crackers for lunch; pineapple juice and pecans for a snack. *If you eat only the foods on your diet, you'll earn six stars a day to paste on your chart. And each night at bedtime, you'll win a prize.*"

"Goody, goody," said Mary.

"And at the end of about two weeks," continued Mama, "if you stay on your diet and don't cheat, you'll win a *big* prize."

We're going to play a diet game. You can win prizes.

You can earn six stars every day.

Here's your prize for earning six stars today.

Mary, you finished your diet! Here's your big prize.

A ROTATED DIET HELPS

Variety is the spice of life, and a rotated-diversified diet will help you manage your child's hidden allergies.

A rotated diet is a varied and carefully planned diet. Your child eats different foods every day and he doesn't repeat a food any more than every 4 to 7 days.

Rotating your child's diet isn't easy. Yet, if your child and your family are loaded with allergies, a rotated (or rotary-diversified) diet can help you treat present food allergies and prevent others from developing in the future.

ROTATED DIETS

FOOD	DAY			
	1	**2**	**3**	**4**
Meats	Beef	Chicken	Shrimp	Trout
Fruits	Orange	Banana	Pineapple	Apple
Vegetables	White potato	Sweet Potato	Carrot	Squash
Grains	Wheat	Amaranth	Rice	Buckwheat
Nuts	Pecan	Almond	Cashew	Filbert
Fats & Oils	Butter	Safflower oil	Walnut oil	Sunflower oil
Miscellaneous	Milk	Egg	Chocolate	Carob

Yeasts and the Yeast Connection

Yeasts are single-cell microorganisms which belong to the vegetable kingdom, and like their cousins the molds, they live all around you. One family of yeasts, *Candida albicans*,* normally lives in your child's body and more especially in his digestive tract. As you probably know, *Candida albicans* is the most common cause of vaginal yeast infections. It also causes thrush, persistent diaper rashes and digestive upsets in infants and young children.

In discussing yeasts, John Willard Rippon, Ph.D.**, of the University of Chicago, said in effect,

> "Yeasts (including *Candida albicans*) are mild-mannered creatures incapable of producing infection in a normal, healthy individual. They only cause trouble in the person with weakened defenses."

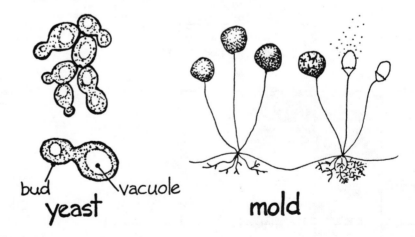

bud vacuole
yeast   mold

---

*See also Part III, "Overcoming Yeast-Connected Hyperactivity."
**Rippon, J. W.: *Medical Mycology* (2nd Ed.), Philadelphia, W. B. Saunders, 1982.

Accordingly, candida may cause serious infections in people who have received organ transplants and who have taken prolonged courses of immunosuppressive drugs. It also causes problems in people with cancer, AIDS and other disorders which profoundly effect the immune system.

The relationship of *Candida albicans* to many other common health disorders was first described by C. Orian Truss, M.D. This Birmingham, Alabama, physician told how a sugar-free special diet and the antifungal medication nystatin helped many of his sick patients get well. Although Truss, an internist, dealt mainly with adults with fatigue, depression, PMS and other health problems of women, he also noted that recurrent ear infections and nervous system symptoms in children were often yeast related.*

Dr. C. Orian Truss first noted that recurrent ear infections and nervous symptoms in children were yeast related.

In his book, *The Missing Diagnosis*, Truss made these comments:

> "The problem of chronic candidiasis in infants and children is especially important, not only as it relates to their health at this period of their lives, but also as it may relate to problems with yeast later in life."

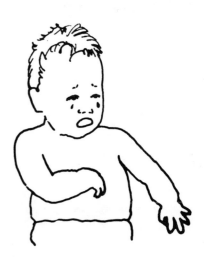

Truss described in detail his experiences with a 16-month-old male child who was seen because of almost constant health problems that began at 2½ months of age. The ensuing year the child had repeated ear infections and received Keflex and other antibiotic drugs. At 10 months tubes were put in his ears, yet, the episodes of otitis continued. He was also troubled by constant irritability and sleeping problems.

---

*Truss, C. O.: *The Missing Diagnosis*, pages 77-82, P. O. Box 26508, Birmingham, AL 35226, 1983.

The child was placed on oral nystatin, which was continued for four months. During this time, he remained completely well. Commenting on his experiences with this patient, Truss noted,

> "In my opinion, this is not an isolated problem. In fact, it is probably very common . . . Perhaps the single most fascinating potentially important aspect of this case was the abrupt cessation of the ear infections. This suggested that *Candida albicans* was actually causing this problem and makes one wonder about the possible relationship of this yeast to what seems almost a national epidemic of otitis and tubes in the ears."

I first learned about the Truss observations from a patient in 1979 and during the decade of the '80s I helped many, many patients—including children with hyperactivity, attention deficits and recurrent ear infections—with a candida-control treatment program. Here are the two main features of this program: *Avoidance or restriction of sugar and junk foods and antifungal medications.*

In spite of the observations of Dr. Truss and hundreds of other physicians, the yeast connection has been called "speculative and unproven" by the American Academy of Allergy and Immunology. Other critics have labeled it a "fad" disease.

There is, however, "another side of the coin." Here are the statements of physicians who support the relationship of candida in the digestive tract to a diverse group of health problems which affect people of all ages and both sexes.

James Brodsky, M.D.* in the Foreword of the third edition of *The Yeast Connection* said:

"It is time for all physicians and medical scientists to increase their understanding of the relationship between yeast and human illness. Many patients with yeast-related health disorders are being treated ineffectively just because their problem has gone unrecognized. If one reviews the literature carefully, the supporting research is well documented."

Douglas Sandberg, M.D.**:

"This disorder . . . is important. It must be considered in the differential diagnosis of patients with a wide variety of

---

Many patients with yeast-related disorders are being treated ineffectively just because their problem has gone unrecognized.

James Brodsky, M.D.

---

complaints. Since diagnosis at times can be made only through determining response through a therapeutic trial, some patients will have to be treated without a firm diagnosis prior to institution of therapy . . . .

"The potential importance of candida-related illness demands intensive research into all aspects of its diagnosis and treatment."

Robert Skinner, M.D.***:

"Studies at the University of Tennessee indicate that the pathogenesis of seborrheic dermatitis and scalp psoriasis is related to yeast. Double-blind studies indicate improvement of seborrheic dermatitis and scalp psoriasis with antiyeast agents."

---

*Brodsky, James, M.D., Diplomate, American Board of Internal Medicine, Instructor, Georgetown University School of Medicine, American College of Physicians, American Society of Internal Medicine.

**Sandberg, Douglas H., M.D., Professor of Pediatrics, University of Miami. Excerts from a statement, September 22, 1989.

***Skinner, Robert, M.D., Associate Professor of Dermatology, University of Tennessee Health Science Center, Memphis, Tennessee. Excerpt from an abstract of his presentation at the September 1988 Candida Update Conference, Memphis, Tennessee, sponsored by the International Health Foundation, Box 3494, Jackson, Tennessee 38303.

John W. Crayton, M.D.*:

"We studied a group of patients recruited for a research project addressing the relationship between food intolerance and brain function. . . . Symptomatic subjects had significantly higher anticandida antibodies of the IgG and IgA classes compared with controls."

The potential importance of candida-related illness demands intensive research into all aspects of its diagnosis and treatment.

Douglas Sandberg, M.D.

Steven S. Witkin, Ph.D.**, in an article published in 1985 described studies carried out on 50 women with recurrent vaginal yeast infections. He noted that,

"*Candida albicans* infection, often associated with antibiotic-induced alterations in microbial flora, may cause defects in cellular immunity. . . . Recent studies suggest that the infection itself may cause immunosuppression, resulting in recurrences in certain patients. . . . Reports that immunological abnormalities have been reversed following successful antifungal, antibiotic therapy for candida infection lend credence to the idea that these abnormalities can arise as secondary consequences of fungal infection."

*Crayton, John, M.D., Professor of Psyhiatry, Loyola Medical School, Member of the American Psychiatric Association. Excerpts from an abstract of his presentation at the September 1988 Candida Update Conference in Memphis, Tennessee, sponsored by the International Health Foundation, Box 3494, Jackson, Tennessee 38303.
**Witkin, S. S.: "Defective Immune Responses in Patients with Recurrent Candidiasis", *Infections in Medicine*, May/June 1985, pages 129-131.

Ear Infections, Hyperactivity and the Yeast Connection

In the May 1987 issue of *Clinical Pediatrics*, Randi Hagerman, M.D., and Alice Falkenstein, M.Sc.W., from the University of Colorado in Denver and Yeshiva University in New York, published an interesting study in which they reported a clear relationship between ear infections and hyperactivity. Here are some excerpts from

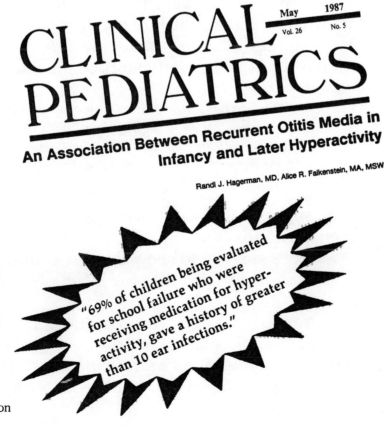

CLINICAL PEDIATRICS

May 1987 Vol. 26 No. 5

An Association Between Recurrent Otitis Media in Infancy and Later Hyperactivity

Randi J. Hagerman, MD, Alice R. Falkenstein, MA, MSW

"69% of children being evaluated for school failure who were receiving medication for hyperactivity, gave a history of greater than 10 ear infections."

Used with permission

an abstract of their article which appeared in the November 1987 *Parents Pediatric Report:*

> "Ear infections and their effect on language development are a prominent topic in the pediatric literature. Hyperactivity has also been a hot item, of interest not only to pediatricians but also to parents, educators, daycare personnel and anyone who interacts with children. On the surface they seem to be two unrelated entities. But could there be a connection between these two conditions? Very much so, says a study from the University of Colorado in Denver and Yeshiva University in New York."

These investigators found that 89% of the hyperactive children they studied gave a history of 3 or more ear infections. Moreover, 74% of these children experienced more than 10 ear infections. Of the severely hyperactive children (those requiring medication) 94% had 3 or more ear infections and 69% had more than 10 infections.

A Japanese researcher found that a toxin from Candida albicans caused immunosuppression.

Then they compared these findings to non-hyperactive children. Only 50% of non-hyperactive children had 3 or more ear infections, and only 20% had more than 10 ear infections. The investigators commented:

> "When these facts are subjected to critical statistical analysis, they show *a highly significant association between early ear infections and the subsequent development of hyperactivity.* However, how these two conditions are linked together is just not known."

They suggested further investigation of this interesting phenomenon.

Here's support to show that the common yeast, *Candida albicans,* is related to ear infections and hyperactivity.

Over 20 years ago, Kazuo Iwata, M.D. (Chairman and Professor of Microbiology, Meiji College of Pharmacy, Tokyo), began studying *Candida albicans.* Along with coworkers Iwata successfully isolated a potent, lethal toxin,

canditoxin, from a virulent strain of *Candida albicans*.*
Iwata found that injecting these toxins into mice caused
immunosuppression, irritability and other severe systemic and nervous symptoms.

Repeated or prolonged administration of broad-
spectrum antibiotics is associated with alterations in microbial flora, resulting in the overgrowth of candida. The
research studies of Steven S. Witkin, Ph.D.**, show that
these changes may cause defects in cellular immunity
leading to further infections.

Observations by W. A. Walker, M.D.*** of Harvard and
others show that when the mucous barrier of the gut is ir-
ritated or compromised, enterotoxins and ingested food allergens are apt to penetrate the intestinal surface and
cause adverse reactions.

The observations of many physicians****, and my
own observations*****, show that *hyperactivity in most
children is diet-related.*

So to summarize:

1. Ear infections are treated with antibiotic drugs
   which wipe out normal gut flora.
2. Candida overgrows and produces toxins which
   weaken the immune system.

*Iwata, K. and Yamamoto, Y.: "Glycoprotein Toxins Produced by *Candida Albicans*", *Pro-
ceedings of the Fourth International Conference on the Mycoses,* June 1977, PAHO Scien-
tific Publication #356.
**Witkin, S. S.: *Infections In Medicine,* May/June 1985, pp.129-32.
***Walker, W. A.: in Brostroff, J. & Challacombe, S. J.: *Food Allergy and Intolerance,* Lon-
don, Balliere & Tindall, 1987. pp. 209.
****Egger, J. et al: "Controlled Trial of Oligoantigenic Treatment (elimination diet) in the
Hyperkinetic Syndrome," *The Lancet,* March 9, 1985. 1 (8428) 540-45.
*****Crook, W. G.: "Can What A Child Eats Make Him Dull, Hyperactive or Stupid?"
Journal of Learning Disabilities, 13:281-286, 1980.

3. More ear infections develop; more antibiotics are given. A vicious cycle develops.
4. The lining of the gut is weakened and more food allergens get into the blood stream.
5. Food allergens cause nervous system symptoms in most hyperactive children.
6. Candida toxins also affect the nervous system.

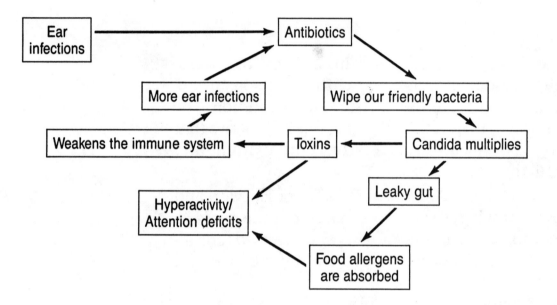

Psychological Vitamins

Juanita and Alfonso, the parents of six-year-old José, said, "Of course we love him, he's our child. But his behavior is such that it's hard for us—or for anyone—to like him!"

During my visit with Jose's parents, I said, "I understand. I can see how his overactive, irritable, obnoxious behavior can drive you up the wall. Yet, I'm certain José will improve when you clean up his diet and take the other steps we've discussed—including providing him with psychological vitamins."

Here Are Suggestions

1. *Spend time with your child*—quality time. In his book, *Raising Positive Kids in a Negative World,** Zig Ziglar,

> **"The one thing that upset children the most was spending too little time with their parents."**   **Zig Ziglar**

in the chapter entitled "For a Child Love is Spelled T-I-M-E", told about a study involving 2,500 fifth graders. The study showed that "the one thing that upset children the most was spending too little time with their parents."

Also, while "quality time" is important, Ziglar said,

> "There's no way you can sit down with your child and say, 'Okay, now let's have ten minutes of quality time.' Instead, it could mean a leisurely but informative afternoon at the zoo or at a museum.

---

*Ziglar, Z.: *Raising Positive Kids in a Negative World,* Nashville and New York, Thomas Nelson Publishers, 1985.

"It could be a family picnic where all members of the family participate in preparing the foods, choosing the location, planning activities for before and after the meal. It could be a trip to a nearby historical site or a walk in the park or neighborhood."

2. *Smile at him and notice him*—especially when he's sitting still or staying out of trouble.* As Spencer Johnson talked about in his books *One Minute Father* and *One Minute Mother*,** "Catch him doing something right."

3. *Touch, hold, pat and pet him*. Physical contact stimulates the release of endorphins, a chemical which lessens irritability, nervousness, anxiety and pain.

In his book *Touching*, Ashley Montagu told of scientific studies with rats:

"The more handling and petting the rats received, the better they did in laboratory situations. . . . Equally remarkable was the influence of gentle handling upon behavioral development. And such handling produced gentle, unexcitable animals."

Some years ago, several California pediatricians described their experiences in treating 24 hyperactive children without drugs. The doctors said, "We've now treated 24 hyperactive children with good results. Our treatment program consists mainly of massage for relaxation of muscle tension or talking to the child in a soothing tone."

---

*Additional information on behavior modification and other ways of helping children with attention deficits (with and without hyperactivity) can be found in publications and audio tapes by Edna D. Copeland, Ph.D., P.O. Box 12389, Atlanta, GA 30355-2389. (404) 256-0903

**Johnson, S.: *One Minute Mother*, New York: William Morrow, 1983, page 47.

4. *Give him simple jobs that will make him feel useful*—things that you know he can complete successfully. And when he finishes the task, reward him. A word of sincere praise will usually mean more than a tangible gift, although both types of awards can be appropriate.

   For example, ask your child to help you bring in the groceries, set the table or pick up newspapers from the floor in the family room. As he becomes more confident, give him tasks that challenge him. But don't make them so difficult that he'll become discouraged.

5. *Praise him.* Praising your hyperactive, irritable child (like watering a drooping rose bush) will help him "bloom." When you praise, be specific.* When he cleans up the family room, don't just tell him what a good boy he is. Instead, let him know that you appreciated his stacking the books neatly on the shelf and putting his toys back in the toy box.

   According to Zig Ziglar, "My friend Cavett Robert said that three billion people go to bed hungry every night, but that 4 billion people go to bed hungry for praise or appreciation every night." Ziglar then lists 100 ways to say "very good" which teachers of his "I CAN" course use in their classrooms. Here are a few of them:

   > Good for you! I like that. Nice going. That's much better. Now you have it. That's the way to do it! Good job! Terrific! Super! Beautifully done.

---

*When he does something you don't approve of, the same rule applies. Make sure it's the behavior, not the child, you condemn.

6. *Avoid loaded praise.* Here are examples:

"The picture is beautiful, but wouldn't it look better if you put the tree over there?"

"The B you made in Reading is good. Next time try to get an A."

Such remarks frustrate your child and make him feel he hasn't measured up.

7. *Be consistent.* Some parents dish out praise only when *they're* feeling good. Base your praise on your child's behavior, not on your mood.

8. *Be patient.* Try to think patient, happy thoughts (difficult though it may be!) when you're dealing with your child. Children are "parent watchers" and can sense their emotions. Even though you say pleasant words, if you're thinking, "I'd like to ring his neck," he'll read your body language.

Psychological vitamins help—they really do.

Remember, your child doesn't want to appear "bad," clumsy or inept. It will take time for him to overcome the nutritional, allergic (and other) imbalances that contribute to his annoying and frustrating behavior. So even though he doesn't immediately respond to the psychological vitamins you're giving him, don't be discouraged. They help—they really do!

Management and Discipline

During the past 40 years, I've examined and treated thousands of children with behavior, discipline and learning problems. I've also counseled their parents and visited with their teachers.

I'm not claiming to have solved the problems in all of these children. Yet, I've seen dramatic changes in children's behavior (and other mental and nervous symptoms) by applying the principles outlined in this book. Here are a few examples:

Sarah, a 7-month-old totally breast-fed infant, cried, slept poorly and was hard to manage until Sarah's mother eliminated cow's milk from her own diet.

Jeffrey, a 9-month-old child who never slept, thrashed around in his bed and cried so much that his parents finally put him in their bed; there he slept soundly. Their conclusion: "He's spoiled."

After Jeffrey wore out the odorous plastic cover on his mattress, the parents purchased a new mattress cover made from cotton. Following this change the sleep problem vanished.

Melanie, an 18-month-old irritable child, was bothered by almost constant nasal congestion—especially at night. Her congestion and restless sleep disappeared when polyester sheets and gowns were replaced by cotton.

John, a 7-month-old, had experienced repeated ear infections. Even after his ear infections cleared, he remained crabby and irritable. His respiratory and nervous-system symptoms cleared dramatically when he was placed on small doses of nystatin, three times daily for several months.

Neil experienced problems almost from birth. Crying, irritability, rhinitis, digestive symptoms, unhappiness and delayed development. At the age of 3, consultants at a child development center told his parents that he was mentally retarded. Following the elimination of milk, chocolate, egg, chicken and several other foods, his symptoms vanished. Neil, now in his twenties, recently received his masters degree from the University of Tennessee.

Two-and-a-half-year-old Charlie was expelled from a church nursery school in Memphis because of aggressive and generally obnoxious behavior. Upon the elimination of red dye, milk, peanuts and other foods, he showed a dramatic change in personality. Today he's in the 11th grade and according to his mother, "He's given me less trouble than any of my four children."

Twenty years ago, David was expelled from kindergarten because of hyperactivity, irritability and uncooperative behavior. Following the removal of corn and other allergy troublemaking foods, his behavior and nervous symptoms improved dramatically. Today, in his twenties, David has completed college and theological school and is pastor of a church in Parker, Arkansas.

Experiences with these children and countless others are the reason I emphasize the role of nutritional, allergic, metabolic, environmental and toxic causes of nervous system symptoms in infants and children.

If your child is difficult, aggressive and demanding in spite of following the recommendations in this book, the following publications may provide you with additional information and help.

Parents' Survival Handbook* by L. Eugene Arnold, M. Ed., M.D., professor of psychiatry, Ohio State University. This book by a child psychiatrist, educator and father of five children provides parents with a readable distillation

---

A good boss is pleasant . . . makes the rules and expectations clear.
L. Eugene Arnold, M.Ed., M.D.

---

of practical insights into child rearing. Presented with tongue-in-cheek humor it supports parents in using their common sense on child rearing without feeling guilty. Here are brief excerpts from this book:

> "Parental attention is one of the nutrients children thrive on . . . set up a routine and reserve some specific time for the kids . . . Being a boss does not mean being bossy, harsh, tentative or cantankerous. A good boss is pleasant, looks out for the welfare of his or her underlings . . . makes the rules and expectations clear."

---

*Order from Steve Ramsey, 3286 Kingston Ave., Grove City, OH 43123.

The Difficult Child, by Stanley Turecki, M.D., Diplomate of the American Board of Psychiatry and Neurology, Beth Israel Medical Center, New York, NY. Here are brief excerpts from the introductory chapter:

> "Difficult children are normal . . . They are not emotionally disturbed, mentally ill or brain damaged . . . Difficult children are like this because of their—inborn temperament.
>
> " . . . Difficult children are hard-to-raise . . . Difficult children are not all the same . . . Difficult children make their parents feel angry, inadequate or guilty . . .
>
> " . . . Difficult children can create marital strain, family discord, problems with siblings and end up with emotional problems of their own."

Difficult children can create marital strain, family discord, problems with siblings . . . Stanley Turecki, M.D.

In this book, Turecki offers practical advice for parents of hard-to-raise children. Like Dr. Arnold he stresses the importance of taking charge and regaining adult authority.

Parenting Isn't for Cowards—Dealing Confidently with the Frustrations of Child Rearing, by James C. Dobson, Ph.D. (Word Books, Waco, TX, 1987)

In preparing for this book, Dr. Dobson, through personal interviews and questionnaires, surveyed 35,000 parents. He said in effect:

> "Some children, beginning at birth are very compliant while others are very strong willed . . . The tougher the temperament, the more critical it is to shape his will early in life . . . The philosophy I'm recommending is not born of harshness, it's conceived of love . . .

Some children beginning at birth are very compliant, while others are very strongwilled. James C. Dobson, Ph.D.

> " . . . Challenges to authority will begin at approximately 15 months of age and should be met by love and firmness . . . establish yourself as the leader to whom your child owes obedience. . .

". . . This form of love and discipline has been tested and validated over many centuries of time and it will work for you."

Raising Positive Kids in a Negative World, by Zig Ziglar, Thomas Nelson Publishers, Nashville and New York.

Ziglar, author of 6 books including the bestseller *See You At the Top,* writes practical, inspirational, easy-to-read books for all parents. Although not written specifically for the parents of the hyperactive child, I agree with the reviewer who said,

> "Ziglar's book should be required reading for everyone who has the temerity to try to raise children in today's society."

In a section entitled "Be Careful How You Discipline," Ziglar warns against spanking because of childish immature ways. Yet, he feels that there are times when "an

---

Be careful how you discipline.
Zig Ziglar

---

appropriate application to the backside" is helpful. He also recommends using a "neutral" object such as a wide ruler or yardstick rather than your hand. His main concern is that it must not be a heavy object that would cause injury.

Helping Your Child Succeed In School

Even though your child has a high IQ, he's apt to experience problems succeeding in school. His short attention span interferes with his ability to concentrate and keeps him from carrying out assigned tasks. So he receives criticism from his teacher which causes a loss of self-esteem. He gets discouraged and doesn't try. So the vicious cycle goes on.

Happily, as you identify the dietary (and other) factors that contribute to your child's problems and take the steps outlined in this book, your child will settle down, pay attention and do better work.*

Nevertheless, most hyperactive/inattentive children need special help if they are to succeed in school. Here are suggestions:

1. Don't start your child in kindergarten or school until he's ready (from both the intellectual and behavioral point of view.) Your child may be 6 years old and have

*Solving the Puzzle of Your Hard-to-Raise Child pages 258-266. Ilg, F. L., Ames, L. B. and Baker, S. M.: Child Behavior (New York: Harper & Rowe, 1981)

an IQ of 125. However, if he behaves like a 5-year-old and can't sit still, let him wait a year before he enters school.

Before your child enters kindergarten or school, give him a behavioral test or developmental examination. Such an evaluation helps you decide whether he is truly ready.

2. If you can afford it, put him in a kindergarten or school with smaller classes—very small. This will allow him to receive much-needed individual attention. If he's already in school, one-on-one tutoring is highly effective in helping him keep up (or catch up).

> **One-on-one tutoring is highly effective in helping a child keep up (or catch up).**

---

3. If your child isn't doing well in school, consider having him repeat the grade. International authority Louise Bates Ames, Ph.D., in her 1967 book, *Is Your Child in the Wrong Grade in School?** had this to say:

> "Let's suppose . . . your child is already in school, is not doing well and seems quite clearly overplaced. Should you have him repeat? Our answer would be a resounding 'Yes'. . . The majority of children will accept the notion that they must repeat. . . . if parents and school convey this information in a calm unemotional way.
>
> "Do not talk about failure. Instead, present the position that parents and school made a mistake by starting the child in school before he was ready. Point out that *no wonder* he finds school so hard and doesn't like it and doesn't do well. Say *isn't it lucky* you found out in time so that now he can be in the first, second, third (or whatever) grade again and this time it will be easy and fun.

4. If your child is in school and experiencing problems learning to read, here are suggestions which I've found have helped dozens of my patients overcome reading problems during the last 20 years.
   a. Read to your child and let him read to you.

---

*Ames, L.B.: *Is Your Child in the Wrong Grade in School?* (New York: Harper & Row, 1967).

b. Get copies of Rudolph Flesch's books, *Why Johnny Can't Read* and *Why Johnny Still Can't Read.** Flesch emphasizes the importance of *intensive phonics*** instruction. This means teaching the child the letters of the alphabet and what sounds they stand for.

c. Tutor your child at home using one of these home teaching aids:

   1. *Listen and Learn With Phonics.* (Available from Career Publishing, Inc., 905 Allanson Rd., Mundelein, IL 60060.) This home phonics instruction kit contains illustrated books and audio tapes or records.

*These books can be found in most public libraries.

**You can obtain more information about intensive phonics instruction from the Reading Reform Foundation, 949 Market St., Tacoma, Washington 98402.

2. *At Last! A Reading Method for EVERY CHILD!* by Mary F. Pecci, M.E., and Ernest F. Pecci, M.D. Reviewer Mary Pride, in the *New Book of Home Learning* said, "One of the first books I would really urge you to buy if you're interested in understanding how to teach reading—this book's strong points are:
   a. "The discussion of all known methods of teaching reading."
   b. "Mary Pecci's method itself. She has trimmed the teaching of reading down to seven steps only . . ."
   Available from Pecci Educational Publishers, 440 Davis Court #405, San Francisco, CA 94111. ($24.95 plus $1.00 shipping. CA residents add 6¾% tax.)
3. *Professor of Phonics Gives Sound Advice* and *Soundtrack to Reading.* (Available from Phonics, 1339 E. McMillan St., Cincinnati, OH 45206.)

Vitamins, Minerals and Other Nutritional Supplements

Will nutritional supplements help your hyperactive child? In my opinion, the answer is yes.* Yet, not everyone agrees with me. In a report, "Vitamin Preparations and Dietary Supplements as Therapeutic Agents," published in the April 10, 1987, issue of the *Journal of the American Medical Association*, the Council on Scientific Affairs commented,

> "Application of sound dietary practices should eliminate any need for supplemental vitamins after infancy in essentially all healthy children. In situations in which an individual is unable or unwilling to eat an adequate diet, the physician must decide whether vitamin supplementation is necessary. . . . All health practitioners should repeatedly emphasize a properly selected diet for the primary basis for good nutrition." (JAMA 257: 1929-1936, April 10, 1987.)

*See also Crook, W. G. and Stevens, L. J.: *Solving the Puzzle of Your Hard-to-Raise Child*, pages 166-199.

192

IF a child is healthy . . . really healthy . . .

. . . and eats a truly "good" diet with lots of vegetables, whole grains, fruits, some lean meat, eggs, nuts, seeds, skim milk and yogurt . . .

. . . and if the foods are grown organically on nutritionally rich soils . . .

. . . and he avoids or sharply limits the "junk foods" (refined and processed foods which contain hydrogenated or partially hydrogenated fats and oils) and beverages which are loaded with sugar, phosphates, food coloring and additives. . . .

. . . and isn't exposed to environmental chemicals including tobacco, insecticides, home chemicals, school chemicals, traffic fumes, then. . . .

. . . he doesn't need nutritional supplements.

A number of authorities support the use of supplements in providing "nutritional insurance."

BUT . . .

few children—especially hyperactive, inattentive, allergic children—fulfill these requirements.

Accordingly, I recommend them in addition to a truly good diet. A number of other authorities also support the use of supplements in providing additional "nutritional insurance" and fortifying the body's immune system. These include Sidney M. Baker, M.D. (former Director of the Gesell Institute of Human Development), Jeffrey Bland, Ph.D. (a nutritional biochemist and authority on nutritional education), the late Roger Williams, Ph.D. (University of Texas, Austin), Robert A. Good, M.D., Ph.D. (University of South Florida), and Leo Galland, M.D. (author of *Superimmunity for Kids*).*

In commenting on nutritional supplements, Dr. Baker said,**

> "Vitamins and minerals are not the treatment for behavior problems, but some children with such problems are ex-

---

*Galland, L.: *Superimmunity for Kids* (New York, Dutton, 1988).
**Personal communication, May 1990.

pressing a biochemical quirk which can be remedied by taking supplements.

"Many practitioners 'do not believe in vitamins' therefore, they do not consider the possibility that the child may have a special biochemical abnormality. And a particular vitamin, amino acid, fatty acid or mineral may be required to remedy the problem. Ideally, parents should find a practitioner with skills in evaluating their child from this perspective before simply 'shotgunning' it."

"In my experience the nutrients which are most likely to be abnormal in children with behavior problems are zinc, magnesium, Vitamin B_6, folic acid, certain essential fatty acids, certain essential amino acids and thiamin. The correction of deficiencies of minerals or vitamins (or, more particularly biochemical quirks of nutritional balance) supersedes other forms of diagnosis of treatment.

Many children take in lower than the required amounts of some minerals, vitamins and essential fatty acids.

"A few years ago I would have said that a nutritional deficiency or special need for nutrients must be so infrequent in this country, that looking for it (even in a child with a health or behavior problem) would be a waste of time and money. Such a view grew out of a fundamental misunderstanding about nutrition that persists into the present.

"There are indeed many children in our culture, both rich and poor, who take in lower than the required amounts of nutrients such as magnesium, zinc, some vitamins and essential fatty acids. This, however, is not the main reason why children with behavior problems should be scrutinized from the standpoint of nutritional status.

"The more important issue has to do with *biochemical individuality*. Some people simply have unusual nutritional requirements and they express their unique differences in various ways. In some children it has to do with their capacity to pay attention, and/or focus on mental tasks. In other children it relates to their ability to control or modulate their behavior in acceptable ways."

Here's more. During the decade of the '80s, Stephen S. Schoenthaler, Ph.D., Department of Sociology and Criminal Justice (California State University, Stanislaus), carried out studies in schools and juvenile correctional facilities in a number of states. Here's a summary of his findings and recommendations:

"Collectively the data from our studies show that selected individuals with behavioral, psychological or mood problems are likely to be marginally malnourished and/or suffering from chemical or food sensitivities. The pragmatic solution is straightforward:

"Individuals who suffer from behavioral, psychological or mood problems would be well advised to eat well balanced diets containing adequate fruits, vegetables and whole grain products each day, backed up with a good daily multivitamin mineral supplement, as an insurance policy of adequate nutrition."*

Recently, a scientific study supporting the use of nutritional supplements in children was published in the distinguished British medical journal, *The Lancet.*** In this article, researchers from the Department of Psychology, University College Swansea, SA2 8PP, United Kingdom, and Darland High School, Rossett, Rexham, LL12 OEN, found that *children who took a multivitamin mineral supplement every day for eight months showed a significant increase in nonverbal intelligence.****

*For reprints or additional information contact S. Schoenthaler, Ph.D., Dept. of Sociology and Criminal Justice, California State Univ., Stanislaus, Turlock, CA 95380 or the publication office, *The International Journal of Bio-Social Research*, P. O. Box 1174, Tacoma, WA 98401-1174.

**Benton, D., Roberts, G.: "Effect of Vitamin and Mineral Supplementation on Intelligence of a Sample of School Children, *The Lancet*, 1988; i: 140-143.

***In a subsequent report, Benton reviewed several other studies on the effect of nutritional supplements and dietary changes on children with learning problems. Their conclusion: "The picture that is emerging is a subset of children, consuming a poor diet, who benefit from vitamin/mineral supplementation." *The Lancet*, May 12, 1990, pages 1158-1160. (The 1988 report of Benton and Roberts triggered responses by critics who challenged their findings. Further studies are obviously needed.)

Do these reports indicate that you can give your hyperactive/inattentive child vitamins and allow him to keep on eating sweetened, refined, processed and fabricated food? No, absolutely not.

In discussing the importance of nutrition with me recently, Donald R. Davis, Ph.D., Clayton Foundation Biochemical Institute, University of Texas (Austin), 78712, a long-time associate of the late Roger J. Williams, Ph.D., said,

> "We do not eat enough whole tissues of plants and animals. Instead, 2/3 of the calories we consume come from 'dismembered' or 'partitioned' foods which lack the vital nutrients found in whole foods.
>
> "Our most fundamental goal should be to reduce the consumption of purified sugars, separated fats*, alcohol and milled grains. We need to refocus nutrition education on the benefits of whole foods and the little known pitfalls of dismembered foods. Although I recommend a broad spectrum nutritional supplement, supplements are just supplements and not a practical substitute for good nutrition."

In a Utopian world your child—and every child—would eat a wide variety of nutritious foods grown organically on chemically unpolluted soil. He'd also breathe clean air at home and at school. He'd ride his bicycle on streets free of lead and other chemical pollutants and he'd play ball on fields that had not been treated with lawn chemicals and/or insecticides.

---

*Separated from original whole food source, i.e., butter separated from milk, lard from pigs, oils from corn, soybeans, olives, etc.

BUT . . .

In the real world of the 1990s—in addition to a truly good diet—I recommend "insurance" vitamins, minerals and other nutritional supplements. Those I recommend for most of my hyperactive/inattentive patients contain:

Vitamin A, 2500 to 5000 units daily	Calcium, 250 to 500 mgs.
Vitamin B_1 (Thiamine), 3 to 5 mgs. daily	Magnesium, 200 to 500 mgs.
Vitamin B_2 (Riboflavin), 3 to 5 mgs. daily	Iron, 5 to 15 mgs.
Niacinamide, 20 to 40 mgs. daily	Zinc, 5 to 10 mgs.**
Pantothenic acid, 15 to 125 mgs. daily	Copper, 0.5 to 1 mg.
Vitamin B_6, 3 to 6 mgs. daily*	Manganese, 3 to 5 mgs.
Folic acid, 200 to 400 mcg.	Selenium, 50 to 100 mcgs.
Vitamin B_{12}, 9 to 25 mcg.	Chromium, 100 mcgs.
Vitamin C, 100 to 250 mgs.***	Molybdenum, 25 to 100 mcgs.
Vitamin D, 200 International Units	

When supplements are prescribed by a knowledgeable physician (or other professional), the amounts may vary considerably from those I've outlined. And, his or her experience, expertise and clinical judgement will override my recommendations. Although the use of vitamin/mineral supplements continues to be "controversial" (especially the use of "mega" vitamins) there appears to be increasing interest and support for their use.

---

*Some hyperactive children may benefit from much larger doses of Vitamin B_6—25 to 50 mgs. or more.

**Children who have white spots on their fingernails or other evidence of zinc deficiency may require 15 to 30 mgs. of zinc (or more) for several months.

***I recommend that children with recurrent infections and children who are exposed to environmental chemicals be given larger doses of Vitamin C.

Sources for vitamins and minerals for children include:

Amni Nutritional Products
227 National Ave.
P. O. Box 5012
Hayward, CA 94540-5012
(1-800-356-4791)

Bronson Pharmaceuticals
4526 Rinetti Lane
La Canada, CA 91011-0628.

Cardiovascular Research, Ltd.
1061D Shary Circle
Concord, CA 94518
(415-827-2636)

Freeda Vitamins
38 E. 41st St.
New York, NY 10017
(1-800-777-3737)

Nutri-Cology, Inc.
400 Preda St.
San Leandro, CA 94577
(1-800-545-9960)

Klaire Laboratories, Inc.
P. O. Box 618
Carlsbad, CA 92008
(619-744-9680)

Wellness and Health
    Pharmaceuticals
2800 S. 18th St.
Birmingham, AL 35209
(1-800-227-2627)

Willner Chemist
33 Lexington Ave.
New York, NY 10016
(212-685-0448)

THE ESSENTIAL FATTY ACIDS (EFA's)

You undoubtedly have read and heard that too much fat is bad for you and your children. Yet, there are good fats and oils as well as harmful ones. Bad fats include hydrogenated or partially hydrogenated fats and oils found in hundreds of foods on your supermarket shelf. The good fats are known as essential fatty acids or EFA's. They're found in fish oils and unprocessed vegetable oils.*

The hyperactive/inattentive child usually needs more of the EFA's found in these oils. He's especially apt to need them if he shows any of the following symptoms:

Excessive thirst or insatiable appetite; dry flaking skin; "chicken skin" (bumps on the back of his arms, thighs or cheeks); calluses, brittle, soft or splitting fingernails, eczema or dry unmanageable hair; dandruff; exces-

---

*These vegetable oils are extracted from vegetables, nuts and seeds by methods which do not require the use of heat. They can be found in health food stores and some grocery stores.
*For more information on the good fats and oils, read *Superimmunity for Kids* by Leo Galland (Dutton), pages 5-21, 96-98 and 156 and *Solving the Puzzle of Your Hard-to-Raise Child*, pages 206-217.

sive or hard ear wax; dryness and scaling of the ear canal; asthma and other allergies.

He's also apt to be deficient in EFA's if . . .

. . . he has eaten a lot of margarine, crackers and other snack foods (almost without exception, these foods contain hydrogenated or partially hydrogenated vegetable oils)

. . . he isn't receiving enough "co-factors," B vitamins, vitamin E, zinc and magnesium.

. . . he suffers from yeast-related problems which disturb his fat metabolism.

The supplements of the good EFA's including both "Omega 3 and Omega 6" oils that I recommend for hyperactive, ADD patients, include: Flaxseed oil, 1 to 3 teaspoons a day (occasionally more).

Here are suggestions for the purchase and use of flaxseed oil:

1. Always buy it in sealed, air-tight bottles. Dark bottles are preferable.
2. Always buy dated flaxseed oil.
3. Purchase only in quantities of 8 to 16 oz.
4. Store in the refrigerator or freezer.

Here are U.S. and Canada sources for flaxseed oil:

Allergy Resources, Inc.
745 Powderhorn Dr.
Monument, CO 80132
1-800-USE-FLAX

Arrowhead Mills
P. O. Box 2059
Hereford, TX 79045
806-364-0730

Flora
7400 Fraser Park Dr.
Burnaby, British Columbia
Canada V5J 5B9

NEEDS
527 Charles Ave. 12-A
Syracuse, NY 13209
1-800-634-1380

New Dimensions
16548 E. Laser Dr., Suite A-7
Fountain Hills, AZ 85268

Sisu Enterprises
1734 Broadway, Suite 6
Vancouver, British Columbia
Canada V6J 1Y1

Spectrum Marketing, Inc.
133 Copeland St.
Petaluma, CA 94952

Section III
Still More Information

Helpful Hints and Recipe Ideas for "Cleaning Up" the Diet

KEEP IT SIMPLE, QUICK AND EASY!

Elaborate or difficult recipes can discourage you. As a result, you may fail to successfully change your child's diet.

Meats

Grilled, baked, broiled, or thin-sliced meats—sautéed (cooked quickly in very little oil).

1. When baking meat, add a quick steamed vegetable.
2. Crock-pots can be a friend to a busy parent. Tip: Place frozen meat in pot early in the day. (Meat cooks on the outside first, holding in the natural meat juices.) Add vegetables later or use quick steamed vegetables.
3. For a change, add fruit slices to grilled or broiled meats the last few minutes of cooking.
4. Use onions, garlic and other herbs instead of batters, fats and salts.
5. Slice or chop leftover meats (so they're ready to use) and put them in your freezer. They make good quick hashes, pasta meats, and sandwich meats for the hurried or "tired" times.
6. Avoid processed meats.

Vegetables

1. Buy fresh, in-season produce when available.
2. Scrub well and slice for quick steaming, microwave steaming, microwave steaming, stir-fries, oven bakes, salads or raw relish trays (with or without low-fat dips).
3. Mix with other vegetables and herbs to minimize the use of fat and salt.
4. Bean sprouts and alfalfa sprouts are rich in vitamins and minerals. Children like to grow them at home and they're more apt to eat things they prepare themselves. They're inexpensive and easy to grow.
5. Potatoes, a really good food,can be sliced and used in baked dishes of various sorts.
6. Sweet potatoes are an excellent source of complex carbohydrates.
7. Try some unfamiliar vegetables—squash, turnips, zucchini, etc. Let your children help chop them. Stir-fry is a good way to introduce "strange" vegetables.

Fruits

1. Fresh is best! A word of caution: Many apples (and other fruits) are waxed and may contain alar, pesticides or herbicides. Check with your grocer and find out where they come from. If you're not sure, wash them well or peel them.
2. Slice and use in salads, fruit plates and for dips or plate accents. If the fruit is used as dessert, you may wish to add a low-sugar cookie.
3. Fruit bakes or cobblers with small amount of sweeteners.
4. Use as base for sauces.
5. Use to make frozen ice desserts; also use for snacks.

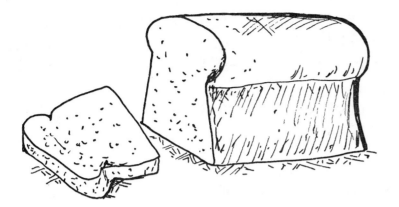

Breads

1. Use whole-grain breads.
2. Whole-grain mixes for muffins, breads, pancakes, cakes and cookies are becoming available in many stores. (On the elimination diet, use rice crackers or quick muffins and flat breads*.)
3. Pastry Poppers—Only one brand that I know of, Nature's Warehouse, is okay for occasional use. It does not contain added sugar and partially hydrogenated fats.

Cereals

Most highly advertised dry cereals are loaded with sugar and many contain artificial coloring. They should be restricted. Happily, things seem to be changing.

Nutritionally oriented companies which offer a wide variety of cereals acceptable to children include Health Valley, Barbara's Ewehorn, Pure and Simple, New Morning and Perky.

Fruit Sweeteners

Several brands of fruit syrups, fruit jellies, spreads and preserves which do not contain sugar are now available. Read the labels!

Artificial Sweeteners

Aspartame (NutraSweet) seems okay for many people to use in limited quantities. It's found in countless commercial foods and beverages. However, some people (including children) show adverse reactions—occasionally serious. Use it sparingly ... if at all.

---

*See recipes in *The Yeast Connection Cookbook* (Jackson, TN Professional Books, 1989).

Saccharin*: This sweetener has been "determined to cause cancer in laboratory animals." In spite of this label, when used in limited quantities, it appears to be relatively safe.

Brand names for pure liquid saccharin include Fa-sweet and Sweeta.

Desserts

1. Gradually, over a period of several weeks, purchase items with less and less sweeteners.
2. Use fresh fruits with one or two cookies or a thin slice of non-icing-type cake.
3. Use "yogurt pops" for kids (young and old) made from low-fat yogurt; and/or pureed fruits frozen in ice trays or popsicle maker. (On the elimination diet, use plain fruits.)

Dairy Products

1. Use low-fat milk and milk products (except with children under 2).
2. Use low-fat cheeses to enhance flavor instead of as "main course." Tip: You'll use less if you grate the cheese and sprinkle over the top instead of using slices of cheese.

Nuts and Seeds

1. Use to enhance and flavor foods or in trail mixes.
2. Avoid nuts that have been processed with fats, sugar and a lot of salt.
3. Remember to finely chop or grind nuts for young children.

---

*For a discussion of artifical sweeteners, see pages 162-164 of *Solving the Puzzle of Your Hard-to-Raise Child.*

Water*

1. Tell your child, "Drink water when you're thirsty." Use other beverages to sip slowly.
2. Keep water cold in the refrigerator.
3. Young children like to get their own water from fun-type containers. Don't criticize water spills. Help your child clean up spills and show him the correct way to use containers. *Keep it pleasant and positive.* Use small cups he can handle easily.

4. Preteens and teens: Lots of water, at least eight, eight-ounce glasses a day helps keep their skin smooth and healthy (when they drink it regularly).

Milk and Dairy Products

If there are no problems with allergies or intolerances, use low-fat milk, sugar-free yogurt or buttermilk. Do not use milk as a substitute for water when thirsty.

---

*Water is often contaminated with chemicals of many types. Yet, evaluating the quality of tap water, bottled water or water filters isn't easy. Here are sources of additional information:

An article in the January 1990 issue of *Consumer Reports*, "Fit to Drink?" provides a comprehensive evaluation of water safety and water filters. Reprints of this article are available for $3 from Consumers Union, 256 Washington St., Mount Vernon, NY 10553.

Two articles in the June 1990 issue of *East West ... The Journal of Natural Health and Living*, are entitled, "Testing the Tap Water," by William Mueller, and "The Shopper's Guide to Bottled Water," by Richard Leviton. To obtain a copy of both of these articles, send $2.00 and a long SASE to *East West*, 17 Station St., Box 1200, Brookline, MA 02147.

Juices

1. Whole fruit is better—more vitamins, fiber and less concentrated amount of simple sugars.
2. Use in limited amounts during the day.
3. Dilute with sparkling water for a soft-drink effect.
4. Add herbal teas to dilute and give a fruited punch effect.

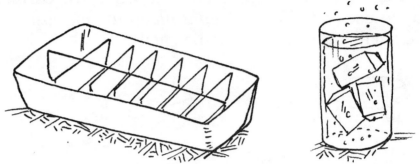

Other Beverages

1. Limit or avoid caffeine-containing drinks; colas (and some other soft drinks), coffee and tea. One cola can be as potent for a child as 4 cups of coffee in an adult. Many soft-drinks also contain chemicals, phosphates, artificial sweeteners and/or sugar. If your child drinks a 10- or 12-ounce soft-drink, he'll take in 6 to 8 teaspoons of sugar.
2. Avoid fruit drinks which are loaded with sugar, food colorings, chemicals and preservatives. (Some of these drinks found on supermarket shelves contain only 5 or 10% juice!)

MORE RECIPE SOURCES

The Yeast Connection Cookbook. Egg-free mayonnaise (Nutty Mayo)—page 208; Oat bran muffins—page 172; dressings and sauces—pages 204-215; muffin, cracker, flat bread and tortilla recipes (these recipes are especially helpful if your child is allergic to wheat, yeast, or corn)—pages 155-175.

The Allergy Self-Help Cookbook by Marjorie H. Jones (Rodale Press). If your child has food allergies you'll find many helpful recipes in this book. Especially recommended are the muffin recipes, pages 97-100.

The Care and Feeding of Healthy Kids by Sara Sloan. This book contains many tips for switching your child over to healthier foods.

Allergy Resources, 195 Huntingdon Beach Dr., Colorado Springs, CO 80921. (719) 488-3630. Excellent source for hard-to-find allergy products, including baking mixes, sweeteners, oils (call to request catalog 1-800-873-3529).

Toxic Food, by Carl Lowe and the Phillip Lief Group. In this 1990 book you'll find a lot of information, including a guide to organic farms and distributors in the United States and Canada. Avon Books, $3.95.

OTHER SUGGESTIONS:

Look for local products and produce grown organically or with minimal chemical application.

Talk to your grocer about special-ordering items for you.

Join a food co-op to help you cut costs and obtain many different and hard-to-get items. You can often get staples, including grains and flours, at bulk prices and divide them among members.

Feeding Your Child—Without Going Crazy!

Jean Smith, R.N., and her husband Clyde (a physician who specializes in Hematology and Oncology) brought their 2 older sons to me 7 or 8 years ago. They said, "Our families are loaded with allergies. We need your help in tracking down the allergic causes of our boys' eczema and their respiratory and nervous symptoms."

After a careful history and physical examination, Jean and I sat down to talk. As was (and still is) my custom, I gave Jean lots of reading material and instructions.

I said, "Begin by getting rid of the junk foods. Then, as soon as you're up to it, carry out a one-week trial elimination diet."

Jean and Clyde followed my advice. (As you might guess, the responsibility was mainly Jean's.) During the next few weeks, she improved the quality of the family diet and identified several food troublemakers.

Since that time, all family members (including twin boys born several years later) have enjoyed excellent health. Thanks to Jean's knowledge and hard work, her 4 boys have required few medications and/or visits to any physician.

BUT . . . accomplishing this wasn't easy!! To learn more about a homemaker's point of view, I interviewed

Jean recently. Here's an edited transcript of our conversation:

WGC: Jean, how did you feel when you first looked at all the diet instructions I dumped in your lap?

JS: *I was overwhelmed—just overwhelmed!* I thought of all the things I had to do and I said to myself, "It's hard enough trying to feed my children—even the things they like. How am I going to get them to cooperate . . . not only the children, but relatives and other people around them?"

WGC: I can understand how you felt . . . And in working with families over the years, I've found that the support, cooperation and encouragement of a spouse is essential.

JS: I agree. It's almost impossible for a person to get things done if the spouse isn't supportive.

WGC: Jean, in the early '80s in dealing with your children, how did you tell them you didn't want them to drink colas or "Tahiti Punch"? Or eat "Sugar Wheatos" or "Chocoberry" cereals?

JS: It was hard. I had to look at my children as individuals and start a teaching process. Yet, sometimes I had to compromise. I would say, "Once a week you can have some of your favorites, whether they're on the list or not."

Today, it's easier. There are more acceptable alternatives—for them and for me. I've also learned more and gained more experience.

WGC: How do you handle things now?

JS: For one thing, I teach my children to look at labels. This way they're learning about the foods that are good for them and the ones that aren't. The older boys have also found out that when they eat a lot of junk food—for example on a Friday night—they don't feel well on Saturday.

WGC: Sounds like a good idea. Could you give me tips for other parents?

JS: Ask your children to help. If you don't, it's three times as hard. Also, don't try to do things all at once.

   If a mother suddenly goes in and cleans out the kitchen and brings in a lot of strange foods the children aren't used to, she's going to have a very resistant family.

WGC: They're gonna say "Yuk"?

JS: Yes. "Yuk—we don't want this." They'll dig in their heels and won't cooperate.

WGC: What you're saying is that you did things gradually without making a big deal out of it.

JS: That's correct. For instance, cookies. When you buy cookies, instead of getting the cream-filled cookies, get wafer cookies. Gradually decrease the amount of sugar over a period of several weeks.

   If you take them off all sugar at once, not only are you going to have a reluctant family, you're going to go through sugar withdrawal, which makes children irritable. You'll become discouraged and so will your child.

WGC: How about soft drinks? Which ones have you found that are acceptable to children, yet don't have coloring, sugar and additives in them?

JS: Over the last 2 or 3 years, several have come out. I use Knudsen Spritzers . . . a juice or juice concentrate combined with sparkling water. Crystal Geyser also has a similar product. So does Sundance.

WGC: And they're about 95% fruit?

JS: Depends on the product. It may range anywhere from 70% to 95%, depending on the strength of the fruit flavor.

WGC: And they don't have coloring or sugar?

JS: They contain no coloring, dyes, or sugars—nothing except the fruit. They can usually be found in health food stores and in some specialty stores and supermarkets. Now there are a couple of lines, Hain and Corr, that do not have the added preservatives and food colorings. However, they're loaded with corn syrup (fructose) and/or sugar.

WGC: How about the little boxes of organic juices?

JS: They're becoming more available. Also, there are boxes that do not use preservatives, food colorings or added dyes. Yet, they do not claim to be organic. They're good for traveling, or when you're going out. However, they *are* more expensive.

WGC: How about tips for snack foods?

JS: I discourage sugary snacks and chips and chip-like snacks. One thing, they're expensive. In the last year or two, better chips have become available—ones that don't have hydrogenated fats, partially hydrogenated fats, colors and additives.

Although I buy them occasionally, I encourage instead, fresh fruits and plain popcorn—not the microwave type. Also, unprocessed nuts for the older boys. Sometimes I make a trail mix for them. I also use raw vegetables, homemade yogurt pops, fruit slushes and whole-grain bread treats.

WGC: Do you have other comments for parents who are just getting started?

JS: Even though you're overwhelmed, don't be discouraged. Keep it simple. Don't let remarks from a friend, neighbor or relative bother you.

You can't learn everything at once. Start with basic meats, vegetables, fruits and whole grains. These products are easy to prepare once you've set up your kitchen.

Doing it this way is easier than shopping for all of the other kinds of confusing products. If you learn on a gradual basis to feed your family with simple foods, things get much less confusing. Don't beat yourself to death emotionally if you don't do things perfectly.

You are stressed and *so are your children,* so find stress relievers. Do something relaxing or fun with your children. Take a walk; play ball, cards, or games; make cookies together. Spend some "non-demanding" time together. Laughing together can make a major difference.

WGC: How about school lunches? Do you send lunch?

JS: Yes, I do. Even though many school lunches appear to be "balanced" they're frequently high in fat, sugar, food colorings and preservatives. It's easier for me to just send their lunch.

WGC: Do they object?

JS: Most of the time they don't, except on burrito day! Every once in a while I'll let them buy lunch. If I use the word "never," it's a red flag. So I use the word "occasionally."

WGC: How often do you go to a fast food restaurant?

JS: Not often—about once a week—occasionally twice. We tell our boys, "We can't do this often. The food is too high in fat, too high in sugar." Even though they're eating it, they know it's a compromise.

WGC: How about Baskin Robbins?

JS: It's Clyde's favorite place. However, the low-fat, low-sugar yogurts have been a big help. Actually we occasionally indulge. It's something we don't do often. Day to day, we eat a basic low-sugar, high-fiber, low-fat diet. And occasionally we splurge.

215

WGC: Were any of your children hyperactive?

JS: They were very active. Not classically "hyperactive." They had short attention spans and you didn't see them sitting down to color. They were constantly moving.

I had one child who was a real restless sleeper, with a hacking cough at night. Another one that just couldn't get control of himself sometimes—crying spells which caused a very difficult time for both of us.

WGC: Did those nervous-system symptoms improve when you changed the diet?

JS: Yes. When we started adding foods back, we found that refined sugars, dyes, preservatives, cokes and chocolate triggered problems. Also milk.

WGC: Could you give advice for the working mother?

JS: Again I say, "Keep it simple." Use your oven. Use your Crockpot. Use what I call a "vegetable bake." Slice vegetables in a glass dish lightly rubbed with vegetable oil or vegetable oil spray. Then I usually flavor the dish with onions or herbs—the children like it.

Put everything in the oven, shut the door and spend some time with your kids. Do what you have to do at home; come back in 45 minutes or an hour and everything is ready.

WGC: Do you have any final words?

JS: Yes. Tracking down hidden food allergies and feeding children a really good diet is getting easier because interest in both of these subjects is coming into the mainstream. Here are a couple of recent examples:

In the April 29, 1990, issue of *The New York Times*, personal-health columnist and science writer Jane Brody talked about food allergies and she said,

"Perhaps the food doesn't have to affect the immune system in order to ignite a yeast infection . . . Certain foods might make some people feel tired or mentally foggy and some send some children into an orbit of hyperactivity."

Then in the June 26, 1990 issue of *Family Circle*, Glenn Plaskin described his interview with Bette Midler. Here are a few excerpts:

"We eat fresh fruits, grains, yogurt, oatmeal, vegetables, chicken, fish, pasta and very little red meat . . . . Nothing processed and nothing from cans."

In discussing her 3-year old daughter Sophie, Bette said, "When Sophie comes home from school telling me all the kids are eating candy bars, I'll say, 'That's fine for them, but that's *not* what we believe in this house.'"

If children are still saying "Yuk," tell them, "Look at what Bette Midler's little girl is eating."

WGC: Jean, thanks a million. You ought to write an entire book for parents. The title might be *Feeding Your Child a Healthy Diet Without Going Crazy!*

Elimination Diets

In my pediatric and allergy practice during the past 30 years, I have seen hundreds of hyperactive, inattentive, irritable children. I've also seen countless other children who were tired, drowsy and depressed. Many of these children were "up" at times and "down" at other times. And most were bothered by other symptoms, including headache, abdominal pain, nasal congestion and bedwetting.

Using a trial elimination diet, the parents and I found that sensitivity reactions to the *foods these children were eating every day were the main cause of their symptoms.* Here's an edited transcript of a tape-recorded visit with two parents of a hyperactive boy.

Parents: Our child is hyperactive!! He talks too much and too loud. He's irritable and doesn't pay attention. He doesn't seem to concentrate although I know he's smart. He also complains of headaches, bellyaches and leg cramps.

    I'm wondering if his symptoms are food related and I'd like to put him on a trial diet. What foods can he eat on such a diet?

WGC: He can eat any meats but bacon, sausage, hot dogs or luncheon meats. Any vegetable but corn. Any fruit but citrus. He can also eat rice crackers and pure oatmeal.

Parents: Anything else?

WGC: Yes. Nuts in shell or unprocessed nuts of any kind.

Parents: That doesn't sound too difficult, although it'll take planning on our part to carry out the diet. What can he drink?

WGC: Water. I especially recommend bottled or filtered water.

Parents: What foods do we need to eliminate?

WGC: Many of his favorite foods. Here's why: The more of a food he eats, the greater are his chances of developing an allergy to that food. Here's a list of the foods. As you'll see, the diet eliminates many foods your child consumes every day including:

Milk, and all dairy products; wheat; corn, corn syrup and corn sweeteners; yeast; peanuts; cane and beet sugar; orange and other citrus fruits; chocolate. This diet also eliminates food coloring, additives and flavorings which are found in many packaged and processed foods.

If your child is sensitive to foods he's eating every day, chances are he may also be sensitive to tobacco, insecticides and environmental chemicals. To gain maximum benefit from your diet detective work, do not smoke in the house or use perfumes, fumigants or other odorous chemicals.

Parents: How do we get started on a diet? What do we do first?

WGC: Prepare menus and purchase foods your child will eat while on the diet. This requires careful planning. When you go shopping, avoid commercially prepared or processed foods. Here's why: Such foods usually contain sugar, wheat, milk, corn, yeast, food coloring and other hidden ingredients which may be causing some of his symptoms.

Discuss the diet with your child and other family members. When you're talking to him, emphasize the foods he *can* eat rather than the foods he must avoid. Study the list of permitted foods and feature those you know he'll like.

You'll need the cooperation of grandparents, brothers, sisters (and other relatives), babysitters, neighbors, teachers, and other school or nursery personnel.

Parents: Tell us more about the diet.

WGC: The diet is divided into two parts:

First, you'll eliminate a number of your child's usual foods to see if his symptoms improve or disappear.

Then, after 5 to 10 days, when his hyperactivity and other symptoms show convincing improvement, have him eat the eliminated foods again—one at a time—and see which foods cause his symptoms to return.

Parents: How will we know the diet is really making a difference?

WGC: By keeping a record of your child's symptoms:

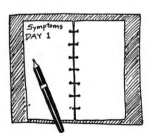

a. for three days (or more) before beginning the diet
b. while he's following the elimination part of the diet (5 to 10 days—occasionally longer)
c. while he's eating the eliminated foods again one food per day

You'll need, of course, to keep a detailed record of all foods that he eats.

Parents: How will he feel on the diet?

WGC: During the first 2 to 4 days of the diet he's apt to feel irritable and hungry and he may not feel satisfied even though he fills up on the permitted foods. He may feel restless and fidgety or tired and droopy. He may also develop a headache or leg cramps.

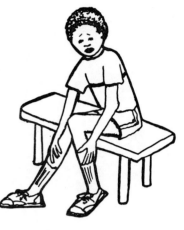

He may be "mad" at you (and the world) because he isn't getting the foods he craves, especially sweets. He may act like a 2-pack-a-day smoker who's quit smoking "cold turkey." Here's why: People who suffer from hidden food allergies are often "addicted" to the foods they're allergic to.

Here's some good news. If the foods your child has avoided are causing his symptoms, he'll usually feel better by the 4th, 5th or 6th day of his diet. Almost always, he'll improve by the 10th day. Occasionally, though, it will take 2 or 3 weeks before his symptoms go away completely.

Parents: If he improves on the diet, what do we do then? When and how do we return the foods to his diet?

WGC: After you're certain that your child feels better and his improvement has lasted for at least 2 days, begin adding foods back to his diet—one at a time. If your child is allergic to one or more of the eliminated foods he will usually develop symptoms when he eats the foods again.

Parents: What symptoms should we look for?

WGC: Usually, but not always, his main symptoms will reappear. He's apt to become more nervous, irritable and hyperactive. And sometimes, the returning symptoms will be much worse than they were before you started experimenting with his diet. He may also show other symptoms, including headache, nasal congestion, abdominal pain or muscle aches.

Parents: How soon will these symptoms appear after he eats a food?

WGC: The symptoms will usually reappear within a few minutes to a few hours. However, sometimes you may not notice a symptom until the next day. Nearly always, if a person avoids an allergy-causing food for a short period—5 to 12 days—he'll develop symptoms promptly when he eats the food again. By contrast, if he avoids the food for 3 or more weeks, his symptoms won't return until he eats the food 2 or 3 days in a row.

Parents: When we return a food to our child's diet does it make any difference what form the food is in?

WGC: Yes! Yes! Yes! *Add the food in pure form.* For example, when you give him wheat, use pure whole wheat (obtainable from a health-food store), rather than bread since bread contains milk and other ingredients. If you're giving him milk, use whole milk rather than ice cream since ice cream contains sugar, corn syrup and other ingredients.

Here are suggestions for returning foods to your child's diet.

Egg: Give him a soft- or hard-boiled egg (or eggs scrambled in pure safflower or sunflower oil).

Citrus: Peel an orange and let your child eat it. You can also give him fresh-squeezed orange juice (do not use frozen or canned orange juice).

Milk: Use whole milk.

Wheat: Get 100% pure whole wheat from your health-food store, add water and cook it. Add sea salt if you wish. If he doesn't like it, try covering the cereal with a banana. You can put the fruit in a blender with a little water and pour it on the cereal like milk or cream. If he won't eat hot cereals, you can use shredded wheat. However, shredded wheat usually contains the additive BHT, which may cause symptoms. So a pure wheat product without additives is better.

Yeast: Use brewer's yeast tablets, baker's yeast or mushrooms. If your child passed the milk challenge you can also give him some moldy cheese.

Food Coloring: Buy a set of McCormick's or French's dyes and colors. Put a half teaspoon of several colors in a glass. Add a teaspoon of the mixture to a glass of water and have him sip on it. If it doesn't bother him, have him drink the whole glass. If he shows a reaction, you'll later need to test the different food dyes separately. Red seems to be the most common offender.

Chocolate: Use Baker's cooking chocolate or Hershey's cocoa powder. You can sweeten it with a little liquid saccharin (Sweeta or Fasweet). Add the powder to water and make a chocolate flavored drink.

Corn: Use fresh corn on the cob, pure corn syrup, grits or hominy. Or you can give him plain, air-popped popcorn (don't use microwave popcorn because it contains other ingredients).

Sugar: Get plain cane sugar. Perhaps the easiest way to do this is to give your child sugar lumps or add the sugar to a glass of water. You can do the same with beet sugar.

Parents: We think we understand what you want us to do. However, a few points aren't clear. Please go over them again.

WGC: Okay, here they are:

1. Carefully review all of your instructions. Plan ahead. Don't start your child on a diet the week before Christmas, Thanksgiving or any holiday. And don't start it when you're visiting friends or relatives. Ask—even beg—other family members to help you. Study your instructions and purchase the foods you'll need. Keep a diary of your child's symptoms for at least 3 days before you start the diet.

   Continue the diet until you're absolutely certain his symptoms have improved and his improvement continues for at least 2 days. Remember his symptoms usually worsen the first 48 to 72 hours on the diet.

   Usually he'll feel better and show fewer symptoms by the 4th or 5th day. However, some children will not show a significant change in symptoms until they follow the diet for 7 to 10 days. And in an occasional child, hidden food allergies won't improve until he avoids foods that bother him for 2 to 3 weeks. However, such a child is the exception.

2. If your child fails to improve after following the diet for 10 to 14 days, "turn him loose." Let him eat what he wants. If his symptoms worsen (including hyperactivity, headache, na-

sal congestion or muscle aches) chances are one or more foods bother him and you'll have to do further detective work.*

3. If your child improves on the diet, return the eliminated foods, one at a time, and see if he develops symptoms. Here's how you go about it:

   a. Add the foods you least suspect first. Save the foods you think are causing problems until later. Remember, your child is apt to be allergic to his favorite foods.

   b. If you have no idea what foods are causing his symptoms, here's a suggested order for returning the foods to his diet:

      1st day—eggs
      2nd day—citrus
      3rd day—yeast
      4th day—wheat
      5th day—milk
      6th day—food coloring
      7th day—chocolate
      8th day—corn
      9th day—sugar

4. Give your child a small amount of the eliminated food for breakfast. If he shows no reaction, give him more of the food a couple of hours later, then more for lunch and in the middle of the afternoon and for supper.

5. Keep the rest of his diet the same while you're carrying out the food challenges. Here's an example: Suppose you gave him egg on the first day of his diet and he showed no reaction. Does this mean he can continue to eat egg? NO. Give him egg only on the day of the challenge and don't give it to him again until you've tested all of the eliminated foods and the diet has been completed.

---

*If your child has asthma or has ever suffered from a severe attack of swelling, hives or other symptoms, do not carry out food challenges—especially with egg (or nuts of any type) unless your physician supervises them.

Here's why: These foods may cause severe and even dangerous reactions.

6. If he shows no symptoms after eating a food the first day, add another food the second day in exactly the same way, giving him all that he wants (unless he shows a reaction).

7. If you think he develops symptoms when he eats a food, but aren't certain, give him more of the food until the symptoms are obvious. But don't make him sick.

8. If your child shows an obvious reaction after eating a food such as severe hyperactivity, irritability, nasal congestion, cough, drowsiness, headache, stomach ache or flushing, do not give him any more of that food. Wait until the reaction subsides (usually 24 to 48 hours) before you add another food.

   If a food really bothers him, you can shorten the reaction by giving Alka-Seltzer Gold in a glass of water (2 tablets for teenagers; 1 tablet for children 6 to 12 and ½ tablet for children 3 to 5). A laxative such as Milk of Magnesia or Epsom salts will also shorten the reaction by rapidly eliminating the offending foods from the intestinal tract.

Parents: Thank you for those explanations. They make sense. Yet, I'm wondering if my child will cooperate and stay on the diet. Do you have suggestions?

WGC: Plan the diet carefully. Discuss it with him ahead of time. Purchase and feature foods he'll like. Don't force him to eat foods he's never liked. Don't worry if his diet is limited. Even if he loses a pound or two, it won't hurt him. He'll soon catch up. Give him a prize each day if he doesn't cheat, then at the end of the diet give him a bigger prize. (See Section II, Helping Your Child Stay on the Diet.)

Equally important, get the cooperation of every family member. If other children in the family insist on desserts or foods not on the diet, don't serve them at the table. Instead, wait until the dieting child has gone to bed.

Parents: Can he follow the diet and still go to school?

WGC: Possibly, if you're sure your child will cooperate and won't cheat. Obviously, you'll have to prepare his lunches at home. However, when you return foods to his diet, it may be wise to keep him at home. Then you can be sure he stays on the diet. More importantly, you can observe reactions when he eats foods he's allergic to.

Parents: We think we understand, but to make sure let us repeat your instructions. You want us to do the elimination diet for 5 to 10 days, keeping a record of our child's symptoms for 3 days *before* we start the diet as well as for the days he's following the diet. Then after we're certain his hyperactivity, attention span and other symptoms have improved, we return the foods to his diet.* We let him eat the eliminated foods one at a time and see which ones bother him and which ones do not. And we continue our records.

WGC: That's right.

---

*Your child may fail to improve significantly on an elimination diet because of offending substances in your home (paint fumes, insecticide sprays, carpet odors, etc.). Before starting on the diet, clean up your child's environment. (See pages 127.) Persistent symptoms may also be caused by sensitivity to foods permitted on this diet, including beef, chicken, oats, rice, or the salicylate containing foods including almonds, apples, apricots, all berries, cherries, tomatoes and other foods. (See page 162.)

Parents: Suppose he completes the diet and we've noted reactions to a couple of foods, yet there are other foods we aren't sure about—what do we do then?

WGC: Keep the foods which caused definite reactions out of his diet indefinitely. And retest the foods you're uncertain about. Here's one way you can do this:

Let him eat a suspected food several days in a row, as for example, Friday, Saturday, Sunday, Monday. and Tuesday. Eliminate the food on Wednesday, Thursday, Friday, Saturday and Sunday. Then load him up with that food on Monday. If he's allergic to it, he should develop symptoms. If he shows no symptoms, chances are he isn't allergic to that food.

Parents: Suppose Johnny shows a reaction when he eats wheat or egg—or when he drinks milk. Does this mean he will always be allergic to these foods?

WGC: Yes, to some degree. And the symptoms will nearly always return if he consumes as much of a food as he did before you put him on the diet.

However, if your child avoids a food he's allergic to for several months, he'll usually regain some tolerance to it. And he may not develop symptoms unless he eats it several days in a row.

Parents: How do we find out?

WGC: By trial and error.

Parents: We're not sure we understand; please explain.

WGC: I'll do my best. When a child avoids a food he's allergic to for several months, he'll generally lose some of his allergy to the food (like a fire that dies down).

For example, if your child is bothered by hyperactivity, stuffed-up nose, headache and short attention span while drinking a quart of milk a day, he may be able to eat an occasional ice cream cone or a cheese sandwich after he's eliminated milk from his diet for several months.

However, suppose he eats the ice cream or cheese or drinks a glass of milk after he's avoided them for a couple of months and shows no reaction. In such a situation, you many say to yourself, "Johnny drank a glass of milk and it didn't bother him so maybe he isn't allergic to milk after all."

But if you start giving him milk every day, within a few days, some of his symptoms will gradually return and before you know it he'll develop the same health problems he had before you eliminated milk.

Parents: But why does a food bother a child on some occasions and not on others? For example, we've heard of milk-allergic children who "kept a cold" all winter and who cleared up when they stopped drinking milk. Yet, they could drink milk in the summertime without symptoms. Why?

WGC: It has to do with what we call "the allergic load."* Part of the problems seems to relate to chilling. It seems to increase a person's susceptibility to food allergies. Also, wintertime heating systems stir up dust and dry out the respiratory membranes and lessen a person's resistance and make him more susceptible to wintertime infections and allergies.

In addition, during the wintertime, your child spends more time indoors. Windows and doors are closed, so there's less ventilation. Accordingly, disease-producing germs are more prevalent. Other factors include indoor air pollutants (tobacco smoke, perfumes, janitorial supplies, and other odorous chemicals). So the combination of food allergies, cold weather, dust sensitivity, cold

*See The Allergy Seesaw in Section II.

germs and chemicals combine to cause many wintertime health problems.

Parents: Do other allergies, such as hay fever due to grass, or bronchitis due to house dust mites, or cat dander, have anything to do with the amount of allergy-causing food my child can eat?

WGC: Yes. The more allergy troublemakers your child is exposed to, the greater are his chances of developing an allergic illness. For example, let's suppose he's allergic to milk*, corn, chocolate, spring grass and house dust. Yet, he isn't severely allergic to any one of these substances. Accordingly, he may play ball in the spring without being bothered by hay fever, and he may be able to eat an occasional piece of cornbread or chocolate birthday cake without symptoms.

But if he eats a sack of popcorn, a candy bar, and drinks a glass of chocolate milk all on the same day after cutting the grass, he may become irritable, nervous and hyperactive. What's more, all these things together may make him develop an attack of asthma.

Parents: I'm beginning to understand more about hidden food allergies. But suppose my child is allergic to eggs and he avoids them for three months. Then I give him an egg for breakfast and it doesn't bother him. How will I know how much and how often I can give him egg in the future?

*See Susie's Cow's Milk Allergy in Section II.

WGC: I'm glad you asked. It'll give me a chance to talk about a rotated diet.* Physicians interested in hidden food allergies have found that their allergic patients who rotate their diets usually get along well and develop fewer new food allergies. *Rotating a diet means eating a food only every 4 to 7 days.* For example, if you find your child is allergic to egg and after avoiding it for several months he eats an egg and it doesn't bother him, you can try giving him an egg once a week and see if he tolerates it. You can do the same with other foods.

Parents: Aren't some foods "kin" to each other—like chicken and egg, wheat and corn or milk and beef? Is a person who is allergic to one food more apt to become sensitive to another food in the same "family"?

WGC: The answer to both of your questions is "yes." Foods are "kin" to each other. Commonly known food families include the grain family, the citrus family and the legume family.* However, recent research studies show that peanut-sensitive individuals usually aren't sensitive to peas and beans and other legumes.

I've found that wheat-sensitive patients are especially apt to become sensitive to corn or rye. So in such patients I'm apt to say, "You'd be smart not to go overboard eating cornbread. And if you eat rye bread every day, you're almost certain to develop an allergy to rye." Although I permit rice

*See Rotated Diets in Section II.

and oats on the diet, if you find you're child is allergic to wheat or corn, experiment further and see if other grains cause reactions.

If he's allergic to grains, here's another suggestion: Go to your health-food store and ask for some buckwheat, quinoa and amaranth. These foods are called "grain alternatives." Although they aren't related to the grains, they contain plenty of protein and complex carbohydrates.

Now for a word about milk and hamburgers. In my experience, most milk-sensitive children can eat hamburgers and other beef products without showing a reaction. However, because cow's milk and hamburger come from the same animal, if milk bothers your child, eliminate beef for a week. Then let him eat it again and see what happens. And if your child is allergic to egg, you can do a similar experiment with chicken.

Is there anything else you need to know? Anything at all?

Parents: Nothing we can think of at the moment. Our heads are spinning. Do you have further suggestions?

WGC: Read, review and study all the instructions I've given you. When you've finished, you'll find that tracking down or detecting your child's hidden food allergies won't be as hard as you thought it would be.

The Yeast Connection

Parents: Tell us more about "the yeast connection." How do you go about making a positive diagnosis. Do tests help?

WGC: No . . . or not much. Here's why: *Candida* organisms are present in every person's body—your child's included. They live on the mucous membranes of his digestive tract, even if he isn't troubled by digestive symptoms. (And they're normally present in the vagina in females.) Accordingly, smears and cultures that show *candida* may not help in making a diagnosis of a candida-related health problem.

Although immune-system tests may help in the study and diagnosis of adults with yeast-connected health disorders, such tests haven't been useful in studying these disorders in children. Accordingly, the diagnosis is based mainly on the child's history.

O - friendly germs
Y - yeast germs
◊ - enemies

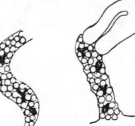

Normal Intestinal
Tract and Vagina

Parents: If tests don't help, what do you do? How can you tell if our child's irritability, short attention span, hyperactivity and other health problems are yeast connected?

WGC: When I see a hyperactive child (or any child with chronic allergic or other health disorders), who has received many courses of broad-spectrum antibacterial drugs, I prescribe an anti-candida treatment program and note the child's response. I call this a "therapeutic trial."

Parents: "Therapeutic trial?" Tell me more about it. . . . What does it consist of?

WGC: It's a treatment program designed to discourage the growth of *Candida* organisms in the child's body. The program consists of two main parts—a special diet and nystatin or other anti-yeast medication. Let's talk about the diet first.

Your child will need to avoid foods that encourage the growth of yeasts in his digestive tract—especially simple sugars and white-flour products. He'll need to feature complex carbohydrates, especially vegetables and whole grains. You can also offer him a variety of other good foods, including chicken, turkey, fish and other seafood, lean meats, eggs and nuts.

Parents: What foods should he avoid?

WGC: Any foods that trigger his symptoms. You'll also need to avoid candies, cake, ice cream, soft drinks and sugar-containing foods of all sorts; also, honey, maple syrup and corn syrup.

Parents: How about fruit juices and fruits?

WGC: Avoid juices, especially those that are canned or frozen, because nearly all contain yeast. Also, during the first ten days of the diet, avoid fruits. Here's why: Fruits and fruit juices are rich in fructose and other carbohydrates that may promote yeast growth. However, as your child improves, experiment with fruits and juices. If they don't cause symptoms, give them in moderation—especially on a rotated basis.

Parents: Other than following the diet, what else do we need to do?

WGC: You can give your child foods and supplements that help control *Candida* overgrowth in his digestive tract. These include garlic and garlic products, and yogurt–especially home-prepared, fruit-free, sugar-free yogurt.* Yogurt contains *Lactobacillus acidophilus.* Powders and capsules containing these bacteria can be obtained from health-food stores. I usually recommend 1/8 to 1/4 teaspoon, once or twice a day.

---

*Some children tolerate yogurt even though other dairy products cause adverse reactions.

An antifungal substance, caprylic acid, is also available in health food stores. Brand names include Capricin, Caprystatin, Candistat-300, Kaprystatin-A and Mycopryl. Although these products are available without a prescription, I feel their use should be supervised by a knowledgeable physician or other professional.

Your child will also need a medication to control yeast organisms in his digestive tract. And I usually prescribe nystatin for my patients with yeast-connected hyperactivity and attention deficits.

Parents: What kind of medicine is nystatin?

WGC: Nystatin is an antifungal drug that kills or arrests the growth of yeast and yeast like fungi. Yet it doesn't affect bacteria and other germs.

Parents: Is nystatin only available by prescription—and what form does it come in?

WGC: Yes. Only on prescription. Although nystatin is available in 500,000-unit oral tablets and as an oral suspension containing 100,000 units per milliliter, I prefer chemically pure nystatin powder.* It contains 500,000 units per ⅛ teaspoon. I prefer the powder for several reasons. The liquid preparations contain sugar and are more expensive and the tablets usually contain food coloring and other additives.*

---

*Available on prescription from Wellness Health and Pharmaceuticals, 2800 S. 18th St., Birmingham, AL 35209 (1-800-227-2627); Freeda Pharmaceuticals, 36 E. 41st St., New York, NY 10017 (212-685-4980); Willner Chemists, 330 Lexington Ave., New York, NY 10157 (212-685-2538) and Bio-Tech, P.O. Box 1992, Fayetteville, AR 72702, (501) 443-9148 or 1-800-345-1129.

A word of caution about nystatin powder. Most pharmacists stock Mycostatin (Squibb). This powder is prepared for use on the skin and is not to be confused with the pure nystatin powder, which is for oral use.

Parents: Does nystatin often cause side effects?

WGC: *Nystatin is an unusually safe medicine . . . safer than any drug physicians prescribe for their patients.* According to the *Physician's Desk Reference* (which provides information on over 2,500 prescription drugs), "Nystatin is virtually nontoxic and nonsensitizing and is well tolerated by all age groups including debilitated infants, even on prolonged administration."

Here's a major reason for the safety of nystatin: Very little is absorbed from the intestinal tract. Accordingly, it helps the child with yeast-related health problems by controlling *candida* in his digestive tract.

Parents: What is the usual dose?

WGC: Most children improve when they take 250,000 to 500,000 units ($1/16$ to $1/8$ teaspoon of the powder, or $1/2$ to 1 tablet) of nystatin four times a day.

Parents: If nystatin helps my child, how long will he have to take it?

WGC: This will depend on his response. He may need to take it for many months . . . or until his immune system and nervous system return to normal.

Parents: How can you tell if the immune and nervous systems are returning to normal?

WGC: By your child's response. If his behavior and other symptoms improve after 2 or 3 months, try reducing the dose of nystatin. If he continues to do well, reduce it further; then discontinue it.

Parents: Suppose the nystatin disagrees with my child or suppose his symptoms continue. Is there a medication other than nystatin which can be used?

WGC: Yes, Diflucan. Like nystatin, it is an antifungal drug which kills yeast and yeast like fungi and doesn't affect other germs. It is a potent valuable drug and in certain ways superior to nystatin. It is absorbed from the intestinal tract and transported by the circulatory system to various parts of the body. So, it not only kills yeast organisms in the digestive tract, but it also helps eradicate them in other tissues.*

Parents: Would I need a prescription? What form does Diflucan come in.

WGC: Yes, you would need a prescription from a licensed MD or DO. Diflucan is available in 50, 100, 150 and 200 mg. tablets. In 1996, a pediatric preparation will become available.

Parents: What is the usual dose and how long will my child need to take it?

WGC: Children with mild problems may respond to 50 mg. once a day for a week then 50 mg. every 2–7 days. A child with more severe problems may require 100 mg. daily for many months. When improvement occurs, the medication can be taken less frequently or discontinued, or the child may be switched over to nystatin or to a non-prescription antiyeast medication.

Probiotics including *Lactobacillus acidophilus* and *Bifidus*, Kyolic and other garlic products, Caprylic acid and citrus seed extract. These products can be obtained without a prescription from a health food store. Their use should be supervised by a licensed and experienced health food clinician or professional.

---

*You'll find a comprehensive discussion of yeast-related health problems in children on pp. 271–302 of my 1995 book, *The Yeast Connection and the Woman*. Also included in this book is a comprehensive discussion of prescription and non-prescription antiyeast medications on pp. 432–483.

Appendix

REFERENCES

Alvarez, W.C.: In Speer, F.: *Allergies of the Nervous System,* Springfield, Illinois, Charles C. Thomas, 1970, pp. ix-xi.

Bahna, S.L. and Heiner, D.C.: *Allergies to Milk,* Springfield, Illinois, Charles C. Thomas, 1980, pp. 67-71.

Clarke, T.W.: "The Relationship of Allergy to Character Problems in Children: A Survey," *Ann. Allergy,* 8:175, 1950.

Crook, W.G., Harrison, W.W., Crawford, S.E., and Emerson, B.S.: "Systemic Manifestations Due to Allergy. Report of Fifty Patients and a Review of the Literature on the Subject," *Pediatrics,* 27:790-799, 1961.

Crook, W.G.: "The Allergic Tension-Fatigue Syndrome." In Speer, F. (ed.): *The Allergic Child,* New York, Hoeber, 1963.

Crook, W.G.: "Adverse Reactions to Food Can Cause Hyperkinesis" (letters), *American Journal of Dis. Child.,* 132:819, 1978.

Crook, W.G.: "The Allergic Tension-Fatigue Syndrome," *Pediatric Annals,* October 1974.

Crook, W.G.: "Food Allergy—the Great Masquerader," *Pediatric Clinics of North America,* 22:227, 1975.

Crook, W.G.: "Can What a Child Eats Make Him Dull, Stupid or Hyperactive?," *Journal of Learning Disabilities,* 13:281, 1980.

Crook, W.G.: "Pediatricians, Antibiotics and Office Practice," *Pediatrics,* Vol. 76 No. 1, July 1985 (letters).

Crook, W.G.: "Controversial Techniques in Allergy," *Pediatrics,* Vol. 83 No. 6, June 1989 (letters).

Daniel 1:1-20, *Good News Bible: The Bible in Today's English Version,* New York, New York, American Bible Society, 1976, pp. 954-955.

Davison, H.M., "Allergy of the Nervous System," *Quarterly Review Allergy,* 6:157, 1952.

Davison, H.M.: "Cerebral Allergy," *Southern Med. J.,* 42:712, 1947.

Deamer, W.C.: "Pediatric Allergy. Some Impressions Gained over a 37-Year Period," *Pediatrics,* 48:930, 1971.

Dees, S.C.: "Neurologic Allergy in Childhood," *Pediatric Clinics of North America,* 1:1017, 1954.

Duke, W.W.: "Food Allergy as a Cause of Illness," *JAMA,* 81:886, 1923.

Egger, J., Carter, C.M., Wilson, J., Soothill, J., et al: "Is Migraine Food Allergy? A Double-Blind Trial of Oligoantigenic Diet Treatment," *Lancet,* 1983, ii:865.

Egger, J., Carter, C.M., Graham, P.J., et al: "Controlled Trial of Oligoantigenic Diet Treatment in the Hyperkinetic Syndrome," *Lancet,* 1985, i:540-5.

Egger, J., et al: "Olioantigenic Diet Treatment of Children with Epilepsy and Migraine," *Journal of Pediatrics,* January 1989, pp. 51-58.

Hagerman, R.J. and Falkenstein, A.R.: "An Association Between Recurrent Otitis Media in Infancy and Later Hyperactivity," *Clinical Pediatrics,* Vol. 26 No. 5, May 1987, pp. 253-257.

Iwata, K. and Yamamoto, Y.: "Glycoprotein Toxins Produced by Candida Albicans," Proceedings of the Fourth International Conference on the Mycoses, June 1977, *PAHO Scientific Publication #356.*

Kaplan, B.J., et al: "Dietary Replacement in Preschool-Aged Hyperactive Boys," *Pediatrics,* Vol. 83 No. 1, January 1989.

Kniker, W.T.: "Deciding the Future for the Practice of Allergy and Immunology," *Annals of Allergy,* 55:106-113, 1985.

Menzies, I.C.: "Disturbed Children: The Role of Food in Chemical Sensitivities, " *Nutrition In Health,* 3:39-54, 1984, Academic Publishers. Printed in Great Britain.

Monro, J., Carini, C., and Brostoff, J.: "Migraine is a Food Allergic Disease," *Lancet,* 1984, ii:719-721.

Oski, F. and Bell, J.D.: *Don't Drink Your Milk,* Wyden Books, 1977, pp. 63-65.

Prinz, R.J., Roberts, W.A., and Hantman, E.: "Dietary Correlates of Hyperactive Behavior in Children," *Journal of Consulting Clinical Psychologists,* 48:769, 1980.

Randolph, T.G.: "Allergies as a Causative Factor of Fatigue, Irritability, and Behavior Problems in Children," *Journal of Pediatrics,* 32:266, 1948.

Rapp, D.J.: "Does Diet Affect Hyperactivity?" *Journal of Learning Disabilities,* 11:56-61, 1978.

Rapp, D.J.: "Elimination Diets and Hyperactivity," *Pediatrics,* 67:937, 1981 (letters).

Rinkel, H.J., Randolph, T.G., and Zeller, M.: *Food Allergy,* Springfield, Illinois, Charles C. Thomas, 1951.

Rowe, A.H.: "Clinical Allergy and the Nervous System," *The Journal of Nervious and Mental Disease,* 99:834, 1944.

Schoenthaler, S.: "The Effect of Sugar on the Treatment and Control of Antisocial Behavior: A Double-Blind Study of an Incarcerated Juvenile Population," *The International Journal for Biosocial Research,* 3:1, 1982.

Shambaugh, G.E., Jr.: "Serious Otitis: Are Tubes the Answer?", *Pediatric Otology,* 5:63, 1983.

Speer, F.: "The Allergic Tension-Fatigue Syndrome in Children," *International Archives of Allergy,* Volume 12, 1958, p. 207.

Speer, F.: *Allergy of the Nervous System,* Springfield, Illinois, Charles C. Thomas, 1980.

Tolber, S.G.: "Food Problems," *Cutis,* 28:360, 1981.

Truss, C.O.: "Tissue Injury Induced by C. Albicans: Mental and Neurologic Manifestations," *Journal of Orthomolecular Psychiatry,* 7:17-37, 1978.

Truss, C.O.: *The Missing Diagnosis,* Post Office Box 26508, Birmingham, Alabama 35226, 1983.

Tunnessen, W., Jr.: *Clini-Pearls,* 2:6, August 1979.

Walker, W.A.: "Role of the Mucosal Barrier in Antigen Handling by the Gut." In Brostoff, J. and Challacombe, S.J.: *Food Allergy and Intolerance,* London, Balliere Tindall, 1987, pp. 209-222.

Witkin, S.: "Defective Immune Responses in Patients with Recurrent Candidiasis," *Infections in Medicine,* May/June 1985, pp. 129-132.

Index

Suggestions for Further Reading

Chronic Fatigue Syndrome and The Yeast Connection

In her Foreword, Carol Jessop, M.D., commented,

> "This book does not claim that the common yeast, *Candida albicans* is *the* cause of CFS; however, it does explain the role of multiple entities: yeast overgrowth, intestinal parasites, unchecked viral infections, food allergies and chemical sensitivities and how these can result in the immune dysregulation we refer to as CFS."

The Yeast Connection Cookbook

If you need more information about the foods you can eat, those you need to avoid and how to prepare them, read Section II (pages 113–359) of this book. You'll find over 200 recipes which will help you prepare foods that you can eat and enjoy. Here are excerpts from Marge's introduction:

> "I've emphasized tasty vegetables of all sorts which will make your diet more enjoyable and less apt to cause allergies. . . . I can't deny that cooking takes time, I can only suggest that *if you really want to enjoy better health, planning and preparing nutritious meals is the place to start.*"

The Yeast Connection Handbook

This 275-page book includes all of the new information found in *The Yeast Connection and the Woman* in a user-friendly form. *Added features include a 59-page chapter which concisely describes the ten steps you'll need to take to regain your health.* Included also are: easier-to-follow diets, meal suggestions, recipes and answers to common questions.

In commenting on this book, James H. Brodsky, M.D., clinical Instructor, Georgetown University Medical Center said,

> "With remarkable simplicity, Dr. Crook gives us an approach to many health problems overlooked by conventional medicine. *It should be read by every person who is not well and unable to find help.*"

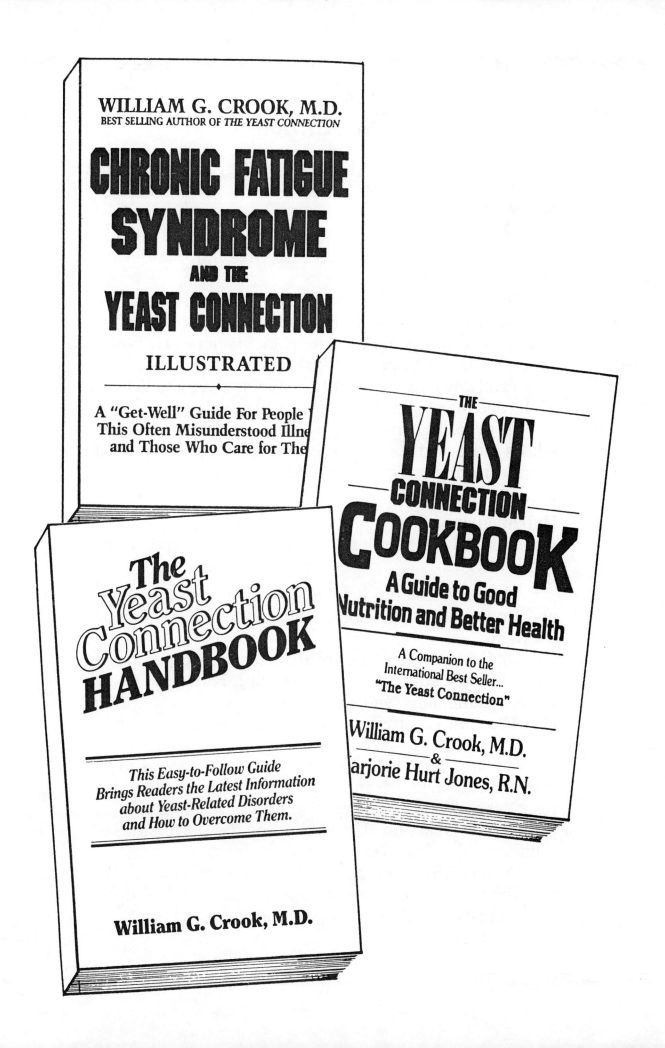

The Author

WILLIAM G. CROOK, M.D., received his medical education and training at the University of Virginia, the Pennsylvania Hospital, Vanderbilt and Johns Hopkins.

He is a Fellow of the American Academy of Pediatrics, the American College of Allergy and Immunology and the American Academy of Environmental Medicine. He is also a member of the American Medical Association, the American Academy of Allergy and Immunology, Alpha Omega Alpha and many other medical organizations.

Dr. Crook is a practicing physician and medical writer who is concerned about problems which affect millions of American children. These include:

Repeated Ear Infections   School Dropouts
Hyperactivity   Alcoholism
Attention Deficit Disorder   Drug Abuse and Dependency
Food Allergies   Juvenile Delinquency

This book contains information about these problems and Dr. Crook's suggestions for preventing and overcoming them.

Dr. Crook is the author of 10 books and numerous reports in the medical and lay literature. For 15 years, he wrote a nationally syndicated newspaper column, *Child Care* (General Features and the Los Angeles Times Syndicates).

He has addressed professional and lay groups in 35 states, 6 Canadian provinces, England, Mexico, Australia, New Zealand and Venezuela. He has served as a visiting professor at Ohio State University, and the Universities of California (San Francisco) and Saskatchewan.

Dr. Crook lives in Jackson, Tennessee with his wife Betsy. They have three daughters and four grandchildren. His interests include golf, oil painting and travel.